Controlling
PEOPLE

The Paradoxical Nature
of Being Human

Richard S. Marken and Timothy A. Carey

AUSTRALIANACADEMIC**PRESS**

First published 2015 by:
Australian Academic Press Group Pty. Ltd.
18 Victor Russell Drive
Samford Valley QLD 4520, Australia
www.australianacademicpress.com.au

National Library of Australia Cataloguing-in-Publication entry :

Creator: Marken, Richard S., author.

Title: Controlling people: the paradoxical nature of being human
/ Richard S. Marken, Timothy A. Carey.

ISBN   9781922117649 (paperback)
ISBN   9781922117656 (ebook)

Subjects: Control (Psychology)
                                     Perceptual control theory.
                                     Human behavior.

Other Creators/Contributors: Carey, Timothy A., author.

Dewey Number: 158.2

Publisher & Copy Editor: Stephen May

Cover design: Maria Biaggini, The Letter Tree

Page design & typesetting: Australian Academic Press

Printing: Lightning Source

Contents

Preface

When you hear that a person is 'controlling' what might first come to mind is someone who is very manipulative, such as an authoritarian parent or an overbearing boss. But what might also come to mind is someone who is very skillful, such as a baseball pitcher with 'good control', or a race car driver expertly steering their high performance vehicle through a tight turn at the limits of adhesion.

What these people have in common is that they are doing the same thing — they are all controlling. The authoritarian parent and the overbearing boss are doing what the skillful pitcher and the race car driver are doing. They are trying to get things to be the way they want them to be by *controlling* things such as the behavior of a child, the work habits of an employee, the location of a pitch, or the tightness of a turn. Indeed, they are trying to get these things to be the way they *should be*, from their perspective of course. And this is what we all do, all the time, is it not? We are all trying to have the things we care about be the way they *should* be. This book, then, is about the fact that we are all controlling people and that it is completely normal to be one. Indeed, it is just human nature.

But we didn't write this book just to say 'you are a controlling person but that's okay' (although we are going to eventually say that!). We wrote it mainly because we want you to know that your controlling nature can actually work against itself, causing you to *lose control*. This is a paradox, and a challenge for our lives, because our feeling of wellbeing depends on staying in control. We want things to be the way they should be and when they are not — when we lose control — we feel stressed, depressed, or anxious. Yet our efforts to be in control are often the reason we lose it.

Losing control happens when we try to control what we shouldn't control, which is usually people's behavior (including our own, since we are people too). This paradox is reflected in the title of this book, which refers to people who are controlling and to people who control people. The paradox of being a controlling person is that when we try to control people (both ourselves and others) we risk losing control because other people are also seeking control over what they care about (including themselves and us).

The obvious solution to this paradox would seem to be to stop trying to control people. But we will see that this is not in fact a solution. It won't work because controlling is as essential to our existence as breathing. That's why there is a paradox. We can no more stop trying to control people — especially people who are doing everything wrong from our perspective — than we can hold our breath indefinitely.

So how do we cope with the paradox we are placed in by our controlling nature? The aim of this book is to show you how. The short answer is that you do it by coming to understand and accept yours and other people's controlling nature. Doing this involves knowing what controlling is, how it works, and why you can lose control when you try to control other people who are trying to be in control just like you are.

The first chapters of this book explain what controlling is. We will show you that controlling is just a more technical way of describing what you are already familiar with as purposeful or goal-oriented behavior. People who are controlling are simply acting to achieve their purposes or goals. But viewing purposeful behavior as controlling makes us aware of the fact that we are consistently achieving our goals in a constantly and unpredictably changing world that should make such consistency impossible. So we will see that purposeful behavior, *controlling*, involves varying our actions in just the right way so that we are able to achieve our goals in a world that sometimes seems to be working against us.

The next chapters are about how this controlling works. They describe how the brain and nervous system allow you to act appropriately to consistently achieve your goals in an unpredictably changing world. We will show that your brain does this by specifying the goals to be achieved rather than the actions that should be used to achieve them.

Chapters 6 and 7 explain why people lose control when they try to control other people. The basic problem is conflict, where people literally end up at 'cross purposes' with each other (or themselves) so that no one is able to achieve their goals. We then describe a way to get out of conflicts when you find yourself in them. We will show that while it is virtually impossible to avoid all conflicts, it is possible — and rather easy — to 'rise above them' and get them to literally disappear. When conflicts disappear your ability to be 'in control' and your sense of wellbeing suddenly reappears.

In the final chapters of the book we speculate about how groups of controlling people — societies — can organize themselves in ways that maximize everyone's ability to be in control and minimize the conflicts that prevent this.

The ideas presented in this book are based on the work of William T. Powers, who was the first to recognize that we are all controlling people. Powers developed a theory to explain the controlling that people do. The theory, which is now called Perceptual Control Theory (PCT), is described in his classic text *Behavior: The Control of Perception*[1]. PCT is an explanation of how controlling people 'work' but it can also be considered a theory of human behavior in general because, as we shall see, behaving *is* controlling. PCT explains how we do everything we do, from balancing on two sticks attached to rubber bands (our legs) to solving differential equations; from taking a sip of tea to writing a book about controlling. But most importantly, given the aim of this book, PCT explains why it is human nature for people to want to be in control and why controlling itself can result in the loss of control.

PCT is an important and revolutionary approach to understanding human nature. Therefore, it should be of interest to anyone who wants to achieve a more effective and fulfilling life through self-knowledge. But PCT is a scientific theory, so most of what is written about it is fairly technical and, thus, accessible only to those with the technical skills that are required to understand it. This book is an attempt to bring PCT to a more general audience. And to do so in a way that shows its very practical implications. We believe that the level of understanding of PCT that you can get from this book will provide you with the basic tools needed to be a more effective controlling person who better understands, and is more tolerant of, your own controlling and that of the controlling people around you.

About the Authors

Dr Richard S. Marken is a research psychologist, human factors engineer, and statistical consultant. He received his BA in psychology (cum laude) from UCLA and his Ph.D in experimental psychology from UCSB. Richard was Associate Professor and Chairman of the Department of Psychology at Augsburg College in Minneapolis, Minnesota. He also consulted at Honeywell, Inc. on statistical, methodological, and human factors issues related to workspace design and human–computer interface technology. Richard had a 15-year career as an Engineering Specialist at The Aerospace Corporation in El Segundo, California where he developed methods for rapidly prototyping and evaluating designs for the human–computer interface component of satellite ground control systems. He then spent 5 years as a Senior Behavioral Scientist at the RAND Corporation in Santa Monica, California where he led research projects on health care quality issues and pilot training system design. He is currently working as a human factors and statistical consultant as well as teaching part-time. He is the author of four books, *Methods in Experimental Psychology*, *Mind Readings: Experimental Studies of Purpose*, *More Mind Readings: Methods and Models in the Study of Purpose*, *Doing Research on Purpose: A Control Theory Approach to Experimental Psychology* and over 50 papers on control system theory and psychology.

Professor Timothy A. Carey is a psychologist specialising in clinical psychology with a background in teaching including preschools, special education, and behavior management. He has worked in a secure psychiatric hospital, adult correctional facilities, community mental health settings, and private practice. After completing his PhD on the prevalence of countercontrol in primary school settings he worked for five years in the adult primary care service of the National Health Service in Scotland. It was in this position that he developed the Method of Levels (MOL), a cognitive approach to psychotherapy based on Perceptual Control Theory (PCT) working closely with William T. Powers, the developer of PCT, to do so. Since 2010 he has worked at the Centre of Remote Health in Alice Springs and is currently the Director there. He continues to use MOL and to conduct training and supervision in the practice of MOL both nationally and internationally. Tim has over 100 publications including journal articles, books, and book chapters. He also has blogs with *Psychology Today* and *Mad in America* and has used the principles of MOL to develop an app for mobile phones called *MindSurf.*

Chapter 1

We Are All Controlling People

Since this book is about 'controlling people' it seems appropriate to begin with a look at the ideas of one of the most famous of all controlling people, the behavioral psychologist B. F. Skinner. If you think of the definition of a controlling person as someone who is always trying to control other people then Skinner is definitely your poster child. Skinner was a most enthusiastic controller of other people. And, while many of us would prefer not to be thought of as a controlling person, Skinner embraced the title whole-heartedly. Like John Lennon's *Working Class Hero*, Skinner thought a controlling person was 'something' to be. Indeed, Skinner spent his entire career boasting that he was a controlling person and that it was not only possible but a moral imperative to be one. To see why Skinner felt this way we have to take a look at Skinner's ideas about why people behave the way they do.

Selection by Consequences

Skinner's beliefs about human behavior were based on his studies of learning using rats and pigeons as subjects. These studies used his well-known *Skinner box* where his animal subjects had to produce specific responses, such as a bar press or key peck, in order to get fed. Based on these studies,

Skinner concluded that behavior is controlled by environmental events called 'reinforcements' — things such as food, water, and sex. He found that when behaviors are followed by such reinforcements they become more frequent, while other behaviors become less frequent, or stop altogether. They become *extinct*. So, according to Skinner, reinforcements control behavior in the sense that they selectively increase the frequency of the behaviors that produce them. Skinner called this 'selection by consequences' since the reinforcing consequences seemed to be selecting the animal's behavior. Skinner saw the relationship between behavior and consequences as being analogous to natural selection in evolution.[1] Reinforcements appear to select the behaviors that survive and become part of an organism's behavioral repertoire in the same way that the environment selects the organisms that survive and go on to reproduce in evolution.

Skinner assumed that the principle of 'selection by consequences' applied not just to the behavior of rats and pigeons but to that of humans as well. From Skinner's perspective, what people do is determined by the reinforcements that happen to follow certain behaviors. And this is what led Skinner to the idea that it is important to control people's behavior. Skinner realized that, if left to their own devices, naturally occurring reinforcements were as likely to follow good behaviors as bad ones. So the obvious remedy was for people — people, like Skinner, who could distinguish good behavior from bad — to take over the job of arranging the environment so that reinforcements followed only good behaviors. That is, it was a person's responsibility to be a controlling person.

Close Encounters of the Controlling Kind

As you might expect, Skinner's ideas generated quite a bit of controversy and criticism. One of Skinner's most ardent critics was the humanist psychologist Erich Fromm. Fromm rejected the idea that reinforcements control human behavior because it implies that people cannot be held responsible for what they do, whether what they do is write the 9th symphony or carry out the Holocaust. If behavior is controlled by reinforcements then it is the reinforcements that are responsible for these behaviors, not Beethoven or Hitler.

Fromm criticized Skinner's ideas at many conferences, at one of which Skinner himself happened to be present. Skinner described the encounter in his 1983 memoir *A Matter of Consequences*.[2] Skinner was in the audience for a talk Fromm was about to give on how people's behavior could not possibly be controlled. Before the talk, Skinner told a colleague that he planned to answer Fromm's criticisms by controlling Fromm's behavior:

> *On a scrap of paper I wrote 'Watch Fromm's left hand. I am going to shape a chopping motion' and passed it down the table to [another attendee]. Fromm was sitting directly across from the table and speaking mainly to me. I turned my chair slightly so that I could see him out of the corner of my eye. He gesticulated a great deal as he talked, and whenever his left hand came up, I looked straight at him. If he brought the hand down, I nodded and smiled. Within five minutes he was chopping the air so vigorously that his wristwatch kept slipping out over his hand. (pp. 150–151)*

This story may be a slight exaggeration — considering the source — but it is likely that Skinner was, indeed, able to get Fromm to chop the air more than usual. So it looks like

Skinner won the debate without even speaking a word, demonstrating by example that a person's behavior could be controlled by reinforcements, even the behavior of a person who believed that behavior could not be controlled in this way. This was an apparent victory for the idea that human behavior is controlled by reinforcements and a humiliating defeat for those 'non-scientific' enough to believe in human autonomy (or, as Skinner might have said, those who were unable to move 'beyond freedom and dignity').[3]

Despite demonstrations such as this most psychologists — even those of a scientific bent — continued to believe that they could not be controlled. They believed this while also believing that they could control the behavior of the subjects in their experiments. Their belief that they could not be controlled was probably based largely on the feeling common to all of us that we have free will. We feel like we are free to decide whether or not we will do something. We believe that if we were in Fromm's situation we could decide whether or not we would do what Skinner wanted us to do. And, indeed, most of us probably have been in a situation like Fromm's, where we had someone trying to get us to do something that we didn't necessarily want to do. In those situations we feel like we have the choice of doing what the other person wants or not. We know that if we choose to do what the other person wants we may not feel great about it but there will be no fights. If, however, we decide not to do what the other person wants we know that we are likely to be in for a battle. These battles can be very unpleasant so we might allow ourselves to be controlled in order to avoid them. But, still, we feel like we are free to choose whether or not we will 'go along'.

It's impossible to know whether or not Fromm was choosing to allow himself to be controlled by Skinner. But there is a follow-up to the story of the Fromm–Skinner encounter that suggests that Fromm was not just a puppet whose strings were being pulled by Skinner.[4] Apparently, after his talk, Fromm was asked how he felt about Skinner being in the audience. Fromm is reputed to have said that he enjoyed it very much because he was able to keep Skinner's attention by simply moving his left hand up and down occasionally. If this story is true, it suggests that Skinner wasn't the only controlling person in the room. Fromm was apparently doing some controlling of his own. Fromm was controlling Skinner's behavior, getting Skinner to pay attention to the talk, just as Skinner was controlling Fromm's behavior, getting Fromm to chop the air with his hand.

The story of the interaction between Skinner and Fromm suggests that both were 'in control' as much as they were being controlled. That is, it looks like a person who is in control, a *controller*, can be controlled at the same time. Skinner himself saw it that way and called it *reciprocal control*:

> The relation between the controller and the controlled is reciprocal. The scientist in the laboratory, studying the behavior of a pigeon, designs contingencies and observes their effects. His apparatus exerts a conspicuous control on the pigeon, but we must not overlook the control exerted by the pigeon. The behavior of the pigeon has determined the design of the apparatus and the procedures in which it is used.[5]

Although Skinner talked about reciprocal control between people (scientists) and pigeons he would have been comfortable with the idea that it applied to the relationship between people and other people as well.

The Paradox of Controlling People

The idea of reciprocal control seems to create a bit of a paradox of which Skinner was, apparently, unaware. Reciprocal control is paradoxical to the extent that being in control is incompatible with being under control at the same time. This could be called the *paradox of controlling people* since the two meanings of the phrase refer to the apparently incompatible idea of people being both controllers and the objects of control, *controlees*, at the same time.

A nice illustration of the paradox of controlling people was provided by the cover art of the original record album (remember those?) for the musical *My Fair Lady*. In case you don't know the story of *My Fair Lady*, it's about a rather egotistical professor of linguistics, Henry Higgins, who, on a bet, transforms a cockney flower girl, Eliza Dolittle, into a fine lady by teaching her to speak 'proper' English. The cover of the album is a cartoon drawn by the great caricaturist Al Hirschfeld showing Eliza as a marionette being manipulated by Higgins who is also a marionette being manipulated by the playwright, George Bernard Shaw. In this cartoon, Higgins represents the paradox of *controlling people* since he is shown as both controller and controlee at the same time. When we ignore the fact that Higgins is a marionette himself we can see him as being in control of Eliza. But as soon as we pay attention to the fact that Shaw is pulling his strings, Higgins is no longer seen as being in control of Eliza but, rather, as being under control. But we can't really see him both ways at the same time because each way is incompatible with the other; seeing Higgins as in control of Eliza is incompatible with seeing him as controlled by Shaw and seeing him as controlled by Shaw is incompatible with seeing him as in control of Eliza.

The paradox of controlling people is a problem because it suggests that it is impossible for people to be in control and controlled at the same time. But the story of the encounter between Skinner and Fromm suggest that it *is* possible. Like Zeno's paradox of Achilles and the tortoise, which 'proves' that the fleet-footed Achilles can never catch the slow tortoise if the tortoise is given a small head start, the paradox of *controlling people* seems to prove something that we know to be false. Zeno's paradox notwithstanding, Achilles will catch and pass the tortoise no matter the size of the tortoise's head start. And the paradoxical image of Henry Higgins notwithstanding, Skinner and Fromm were in control and under control at the same time.

Behaving is Controlling

The paradox of *controlling people* would eventually be solved by a control engineer named William T. Powers. Powers didn't set out to solve the paradox; indeed, he was probably unaware that such a paradox even existed. But Powers had a keen interest in psychology and his training as a control engineer put him in the position of being able to see something about human behavior that had previously been largely unnoticed. It occurred to Powers that human behavior is equivalent to the behavior of the devices he was building — devices called *control systems*. Both humans and control systems *control*, in the sense that they achieve goals, in a world that often seems to be working to prevent these goals from being achieved. For example, the familiar household thermostat is a control system that achieves the goal of a constant room temperature in a world where constant changes in the temperature outdoors, and the number of people in the room, are working against the thermostat achieving this goal. Similarly, people achieve their goals — even a simple goal such as walking across the street — in a world where constant changes in things like the tilt and roughness of the surface of the street should result in constant trips and falls that work against the person achieving the goal of getting to the other side.

The 'hostile' variations in the state of the world that would prevent control systems from achieving their goals are called *disturbances*. Control systems achieve their goals in spite of these disturbances by acting to counter the potential effects of the disturbances. The thermostat counteracts disturbances by turning a furnace on and off, as necessary. The person walking across the street counteracts disturbances by altering the muscle forces used to take each step. So, both the thermostat and the person walking across the street are controlling, because both are achieving their goals by acting to counter disturbances that would otherwise keep the goals from being achieved.

What Powers observed, then, was that when we see people doing things such as walking across the street (when we see them behaving) we are seeing them controlling. What we refer to as a person's behaviors are the consistently achieved goals of controlling. Indeed, we name behaviors in terms of the goals achieved, and ignore the fact that these goals are achieved by very different means each time. The different means are the actions that are necessary to counter the different distur-bances that would prevent consistent achievement of the goal. So we say that a person 'crosses the street' as though this behavior is simply emitted like light from a light bulb or water from a tap. But Powers, looking at behavior through the eyes of a control engineer, was able to see that behaviors such as 'crossing the street' are not simply emitted. In fact, there is no single behavior, no particular pattern of arm and leg move-ments, that equates to 'crossing the street'. 'Crossing the street', like all other behavior, is an achievement that results from precisely varying actions to counter disturbances that would prevent the behavior from happening consistently. When we see people producing certain behaviors consistently we are seeing them controlling. Behaving is controlling.

We Are All Controlling People

The idea that behaving is controlling doesn't apply just to 'simple' behaviors like 'crossing the street'. Everything people do, everything we call behavior, can be seen to involve control, because all behavior is happening in a world filled with disturbances that vary constantly and unpredictably. We are controlling when we balance a checkbook, get a college education, write a computer application, run for office, or compose a symphony. Each of these behaviors can be seen to involve a goal — a balanced checkbook, a college education, a working application, a successful campaign, a symphony — that is achieved in the face of myriad natural disturbances, such as power failures and pens that run out of ink, as well as those that are 'self-imposed', such as the occasional typing and calculation error. So the idea that behaving is controlling refers to everything we call behavior. People are controlling whenever they are behaving, which is always (even when they seem to be 'doing nothing' — 'doing nothing' is also a behavior). And since all people behave, all people are controlling all the time. This was Powers's surprising conclusion based on looking at behavior through 'control theory glasses': we are all controlling people.

Most people probably don't like to think of themselves as controlling so it may come as an unpleasant shock to hear that you are. It certainly came as a shock to us. But as we learned more about what it means to be a controlling person, we found that being one is not such a bad thing.[6] Indeed, we learned that being a successful controlling person is essential to our psychological health and ultimately our very survival. Because we are controlling people we feel best when we are in control of the things that matter to us. We want to be in control of our income, health, relationships, free time, and so on. That is, we feel best when we are in control of our lives. But, as we mentioned in the Preface, there is also a built-in catch to being a controlling person because our efforts to be in control can also cause us to lose control. This happens when we try to control things that we can't (or shouldn't) control. And one of those things is other people's behavior. This is because other people are controlling people too, just like us, with their own ideas about what they should be doing (controlling). So our efforts to get a person to do what we want will be resisted if what we want is not what they themselves want, and we lose control.

The 'catch' to being a controlling person is that we can't stop doing what causes us to lose control because we can't stop controlling. We can't stop trying to get the world and the people in it to be the way we think they should be. Getting people (including ourselves) to behave as they should is as much a part of being a controlling person as getting our checkbook balanced or our car started in the morning. So, paradoxically, our own controlling nature is, to some extent, the enemy of itself. We can't help trying to be in control, but when we try to control some things, such as other people, we lose control of the very things we are trying to control. This is the paradox of controlling people in a slightly different form. As in the case of the picture of Henry Higgins who seems to be in the impossible position of controlling and being controlled at the same time, people who control what they can't control, such as other people, seem to be in the impossible position of controlling and losing control at the same time.

The paradox of controlling people in both of its guises, like all paradoxes, is a paradox in the mind, not in reality. While it looks like people can't be in control and controlled at the same time, in fact they can. And while it looks like people can't be in control and lose control at the same time, they can. The solution to these paradoxes hinges on understanding our own nature as controlling people. It involves following the ancient Delphic maxim to 'know thyself'. Doing this is not just an academic exercise. By getting to know our own controlling nature we can learn how to live better within it. This means being able to be in control of our own lives without creating problems for ourselves through our own efforts to be in control. It means being able to live in a world filled with other controlling people who are trying to be in control of their lives just like we are. It means having the courage to control what we can control, the serenity to know what we can't, and the wisdom to know the difference.[7]

The first step on the road to achieving this wisdom is to know what controlling is. This means knowing when other people are controlling and, most especially, when we are doing it ourselves. The next chapter is all about how to recognize controlling when it's happening.

Chapter 2

The Nature of Controlling

In Chapter 1 we spent a little time discussing the nature of controlling. Now we'll take a closer look at it. A good place to start is to picture in your mind someone you think of as 'controlling'. Now try to think about why you see that person that way. What does that person do that is controlling? Why do you think of the person as controlling? What we will try to do in this chapter is distill, from this image of a controlling person, the essence of controlling itself.

Images of Controlling

Just as all unhappy families are unhappy in their own way, all *controlling people* control in their own way (with apologies to Tolstoy). So, it is quite likely that everyone has a somewhat different image of what a controlling person does that is controlling. But there are a couple of things that are common. All controlling involves trying to achieve particular ends or *goals*. If, for example, the person you are thinking of is a parent who is always trying to control a child, then you might notice that the parent has the goal of seeing the child perform certain behaviors, such as 'doing their homework'. And all controlling involves taking action to try to achieve a goal. A parent who has the goal of getting their child to do homework might try to achieve it with threats ('No allowance if you don't do your homework!') or bribes ('Extra dessert if you do it.'). If these tactics don't work, the parent's actions may become more intense, with loud pleading, nagging, and cajoling. It is these extreme actions that we see as controlling and we see the person doing them as a controlling person.

The extreme actions taken by people who we see as controlling can give the impression that controlling is rather rough and mean. This is probably why we don't care to be around such people. But most of the controlling that people do is actually rather smooth and gentle. The process of controlling looks rough and mean only when it is not going well. This is certainly the case with the parent who is trying to get their child to do homework. The parent resorts to more and more extreme actions when gentler actions aren't working. When controlling is going well these extreme actions are not needed. If, for example, there were some magic way to get a child to do homework, then the parent's controlling would go much more smoothly. There is no such magic, of course, but if there were we probably wouldn't even see the parent as controlling. For example, it might seem that the parent of a child who likes doing homework isn't doing any controlling at all. The parent and the child might not even be in the same room as each other. The parent might go about the business of watching a favorite television show while the child is in another room completing the homework tasks for the day.

You might however get a sense of the controlling that is going on if you were able to keep observing until the child went to get a drink from the kitchen. Or, perhaps, the child phoned a friend to discuss one of the homework problems and then got talking about another subject, which led to laughter and loud chatter. When either of these things occurs the parent might pause the television show and walk past the child's room to indicate their presence or they might call out from their comfortable place on the sofa: 'Have you finished your homework already?'. The control is actually happening so smoothly and unobtrusively most of the time that it's the disruptions to control that give the best indication that control is occurring.

So, perhaps surprisingly, the controlling that people do is often more obvious when it is failing than when it is successful. As a result, our image of a controlling person is typically of someone who is using extreme and sometimes violent actions to achieve their goals. Yet this image is quite misleading since most of the controlling that people do is quite successful, involving actions that are neither extreme nor violent but rather either hard to notice or virtually invisible.

An example of controlling that is difficult to notice is the example above of the parent who is trying to get their child to do homework. While doing this the parent is controlling many other things about their own physical body, such as their balance and tone of voice. They are controlling their balance in order to remain standing while they yell and gesture at their child. It's hard to notice that sort of controlling because the parent is taking no extreme measures to do it. But in order to keep their balance and remain standing they must constantly shift their weight to compensate for the disturbances to their center of gravity that occur as they gesture and yell. If these subtle weight shifting actions were not being taken, they would fall over after their first finger wag. We don't notice this control because it is occurring smoothly, gently, and effectively.

The fact that the parent is controlling their balance can be exposed by forcing the weight shifting actions that maintain balance to become as extreme as the actions the parent is taking to get the child to do homework. This could be done if we were to suddenly appear on the scene and push them, resulting in very abrupt and possibly awkward movements aimed at regaining their balance (and possibly striking out at the stranger who suddenly appeared and tried to push them over!). The push has suddenly made controlling balance more difficult, requiring extreme actions to regain control. So, again we see that controlling becomes more obvious when it is not going well.

Analyzing Control

Maintaining balance is just one of the many controlling things people do where it's hard to see that controlling is going on. Indeed, as we noted earlier, virtually everything people do involves controlling in the sense that it involves acting to achieve goals in the face of disturbances. People maintain their balance, drive their cars, get their groceries, and prepare their meals (among many other things) quite successfully, and, apparently, effortlessly. Therefore, it's difficult to appreciate the nature of controlling by looking at the controlling that is going on in everyday behavior.

Instead, the best way to understand controlling is to bring it into the lab where it can be taken apart and analyzed under carefully controlled conditions. One of the 'microscopes' that is used to analyze controlling is called a *tracking task*. An example of such a task can be found on the internet[*]. In this particular task two lines, a cursor and a target, are shown on a computer display. In one version of this task, the target is stationary while the cursor is being 'pushed' back and forth by a continuously varying disturbance generated by the computer. The person doing the task is asked to keep the cursor on target by moving the mouse, which can be used to 'push back'

---

[*] *http://www.mindreadings.com/ControlDemo/BasicTrack.html*

against the computer's pushes — the disturbance. This task is much like driving a car down a straight stretch of road on a windy day. The car is equivalent to the cursor and the road is the target. The gusting wind is a disturbance that is equivalent to the computer's pushes on the cursor.

There are two important things that we learn about controlling from an analysis of a tracking task. First, we learn that what people control are things that vary. It is not the cursor itself but the *position* of the cursor that is controlled. Similarly, when we drive down the road it is not the car that is controlled but the position of the car. Things that vary are called *variables.* So controlling involves making the state of a variable — like the position of a cursor or a car — match a *goal state* and keeping it matching, protected from the effects of disturbances. In the tracking task the goal state for the position of the cursor is 'on target' and it is kept there, protected from the effects of the computer generated pushes, by the actions — mouse movements — of the person doing the tracking task. When driving, the goal state for the position of the car is 'in the lane' and it is kept there, protected from the effects of the gusting wind, by the actions — steering wheel movements — of the driver. The variable that is brought to a goal state, and protected from the effects of disturbances, is called a *controlled variable.* So the position of the cursor and the position of the car are both controlled variables.

The second thing we learn from analysis of a tracking task is that you can't keep a controlled variable in a goal state by acting in just any old way. It requires acting very precisely to counter the disturbances to the variable you are controlling. In the tracking task, the position of the cursor will be kept in the goal state — on target — only if mouse movements are very precisely opposed to the disturbance that is pushing on the cursor. The more exactly actions oppose disturbances the better the control is in the sense that the state of the controlled variable stays close to the goal state. When driving down the road, the more precisely steering wheel movements oppose the effects of the wind gusts, the closer the car stays to the center of the lane.

You can get an idea of how important exact opposition to disturbances is if you think of what you have to do to keep your car in its lane while driving in a strong crosswind. When you see the car drifting left you turn the wheel to the right and when you see it drifting right you turn the wheel to the left to keep the car in its lane. But to keep the car in its lane you not only have to turn the wheel in the correct direction but you also have to turn it by exactly the correct amount. If you turn the wheel too much or too little, even if the turn is in the correct direction, you will end up on the shoulder of the road or heading into the median. Moreover, the force of the cross-wind is constantly changing so what constitutes the right amount of wheel turn — the amount that will keep the car in its lane — is constantly changing. But when you are in control of the position of your car you are continuously turning the steering wheel by just the right amount to counter the changing wind gusts and keep the car in its lane. This is remarkable when you realize that you are rarely, if ever, aware of the precise direction and force of the wind gusts that affect the position of your car, yet you are always turning the wheel by just the right amount to oppose the effects of these distur-bances masterfully. Control of car position is usually so good that it can be hard to get a sense of the control that is con-stantly occurring. If you take your hands off the steering wheel (if only for a brief second), however, you'll get a sense of what the car might be doing if it didn't have a controlling agent attached to its steering wheel. Even just thinking of doing this exercise is enough to give most people a sense of how important their controlling efforts are to the ongoing position of their car on the road.

Looking for Control in All the Right Places

We can use the facts about controlling that come from our analysis of the behavior in a tracking task to see when people are controlling in their everyday lives. We will show you how you can look at behavior — your own and others' — to see whether it involves control. Doing this involves looking for evidence that a variable is being brought to a goal state by actions that are precisely opposing disturbances. That is, we have to look at behavior to see if there is evidence of controlled variables.

To make this more concrete, let's start by looking at a common and simple behavior: drinking your morning cup of coffee (or, if you prefer, tea). This behavior involves lifting the cup to your mouth and taking a sip and doing this until there is nothing left in the cup. There are actually many variables being controlled when you do this but the one we will focus on is the destination of the cup each time you lift it to take a sip. The first thing to notice, then, is that the destination of the cup *is* a variable; when you lift the cup it could end up anywhere relative to your mouth. It could end up at your nose, your chin, your forehead, or somewhere in front of your face. So where the cup ends up could vary, but it doesn't; it always ends up at your mouth. And not even at the side or at the top of your mouth. Each time, the cup is brought to around about the middle of your bottom lip. Therefore, you seem to be achieving a goal — getting the cup to your mouth rather than some other place — and you seem to be doing this consistently.

Seeing that a goal is being achieved consistently is a necessary but not a sufficient basis for concluding that a behavior involves control. It is also necessary to see that this consistency is *unexpected*. It is unexpected if there are disturbances present that would prevent such consistency in the absence of actions being taken to precisely counter their effects. And there are disturbances present when you sip your coffee (or tea), though they may be a little tough to notice at first. The most obvious one is the changing weight of the cup as you sip. Each time you take a sip there is less coffee in the cup and, thus, the cup weighs a little less. This disturbance would result in the cup ending up in very different places on each sip if you used the same force to lift the cup each time. When the cup is full you have to lift with more force than when the cup is nearly empty. The forces that you use to lift the cup are the actions you take to achieve the goal of bringing the cup to your mouth. They must not only be stronger or weaker depending on the fullness of the cup but they must be precisely stronger or weaker; too much force when the cup is nearly empty and it ends up on your face rather than in your mouth; too little force when the cup is nearly full and it doesn't get off the table.

What we learn from this little exercise is that when we see a behavior such as 'sipping coffee' we are actually seeing a process of control. In the case of sipping coffee what is being controlled is where the cup ends up on each sip. Where the cup ends up is the *controlled variable*. The *goal state* of this variable is 'at the mouth' and it is being consistently achieved by actions (lifting forces) that precisely compensate for disturbances (the changing weight of the cup) that would otherwise prevent such consistency. In order to see this we have to know a little bit of physics and a little bit of physiology. The physics we have to know is not very deep; we just have to know that more force is needed to lift a full cup than a nearly empty one. And the physiology is also pretty simple; we have to know that the muscles in the arm exert the forces that lift the cup.

Finding the evidence that a particular behavior is a process of control can be difficult at first. But when you learn how to do it, the pay-off is a whole new appreciation for the skill involved in producing the everyday behaviors that we take for granted. You will see that nearly everything that we see as a person's 'behavior' — from making breakfast in the morning to brushing your teeth at night — involves control. You can see this when you are able to look at the behavior in terms of the controlled variable, the goal state of that variable, the disturbances to that variable, and the actions that are precisely canceling the effects of those disturbances.

But it's not necessary to correctly analyze everything people do to see that their behavior involves control. You can get a pretty good sense of the control involved in behavior by imagining what the world would look like if people were no longer there. In his fascinating book *The World Without Us*[1] Alan Weisman does this imagining for us — based on a scientific understanding of the natural disturbances, such as erosion and oxidation, that are always at work — and describes a world where the buildings, bridges, roads, and other products of human ingenuity have literally turned to dust without people there to maintain them. But all these things still stand because the world is populated with people who are constantly acting to oppose the disturbances that would turn everything they care about to dust — a world populated with controlling people. If you look around the environment you currently occupy you'll see truckloads of evidence for the controlling activity of people. It is quite likely that nothing about your environment would be as it is if it wasn't for people's controlling efforts. You can also get a sense of your own controlling if you think about what your appearance would look like in a week's time if you did nothing, not a single thing, to affect your appearance between now and then. Imagine what would be looking back at you from the mirror if you did absolutely nothing to your face, or your clothes, or your hair, or your teeth for an entire seven days.

Controlling as Purposeful Behavior

You may have noticed that our description of controlling could also be a description of *purposeful behavior*. The most obvious similarity is that both involve achieving a goal. When we say that someone is behaving purposefully we mean that the person is working towards a goal, such as getting a job or a college degree. But if working towards a goal were all there were to it, one would have a hard time distinguishing purposeful from non-purposeful behavior. This point was made by the American philosopher William James in *The Principles of Psychology*[2], which is considered by many to be the first psychology textbook. In the following passage, James explains why 'working towards a goal' cannot be the sole basis for identifying purposeful behavior:

> *Romeo wants Juliet as filings want a magnet; and if no obstacles intervene he moves toward her by as straight a line as they. But Romeo and Juliet, if a wall be built between them, do not remain idiotically pressing their faces against its opposite sides like the magnet and the filings with the [obstructing] card. Romeo soon finds a circuitous way, by scaling the wall or otherwise, of touching Juliet's lips directly. With the filings the path is fixed; whether it reaches the end depends on accidents. With the lover it is the end which is fixed, the path may be modified indefinitely.* [3]

James's point here is that both Romeo and the iron filings appear to be working towards a goal (or 'end', as James calls it) so if *working towards a goal* were the sole defining characteristic of purposeful behavior then the behavior of both Romeo and the filings could be called 'purposeful'. But we know that the iron filings' behavior is not really purposeful while Romeo's behavior is. James shows that we can reveal this difference by placing an obstruction in the way of the presumed goal. When we do this we find that the filings stop dead in their tracks while Romeo finds a way around the obstruction (or disturbance). In order to distinguish purposeful from non-purposeful behavior you have to determine not only that the behavior is goal oriented but also that it will 'find a circuitous way' around obstacles in order to achieve the goal.

What James realized is that purposeful behavior is characterized not only by working towards a goal but also by acting as necessary to counter obstructions that would prevent achievement of the goal. The result of this insight is a description of purposeful behavior that is virtually identical to our description of controlling. Since James's 'obstacles' are what we would call 'disturbances', James would define purposeful behavior as achieving goals by acting to counter disturbances that would prevent goal achievement — essentially the same way we describe controlling. James's definition of purpose was not as precise as our concept of control but clearly both terms — purpose and control — point to the same phenomenon — people achieving goals in the face of obstacles (disturbances) that should prevent goal achievement, but don't.

James's textbook could have launched psychology as the science of purposeful behavior but his ideas about the nature of purpose were apparently forgotten soon after they were proposed. This forgetting might have even been a tad willful since 'purpose' has always caused somewhat of an allergic reaction in psychologists — particularly those of a scientific bent. The problem is one of time travel. Purpose implies that a future event (the goal) is the cause of present behavior (the actions that lead to the goal). This seems to violate the Law of Cause and Effect, one of the cornerstones of science, which says that causes must come before — or at least be simultaneous with — effects. So a science of purpose would seem to be a science that is not very scientific.

Nevertheless, human behavior does seem to be purposeful. We certainly think of our own behavior as purposeful. But because it seemed unscientific, many psychologists ended up declaring purposeful behavior to be an illusion. This illusion is that behavior that appears to be caused by a future event — a goal — is actually caused by past or present ones. Romeo's apparently purposeful pursuit of Juliet was seen as being caused by Juliet's attractiveness just as the iron filings' apparently purposeful pursuit of the magnet is caused by the magnet's force field. But this cause–effect explanation of purposeful behavior works only if you ignore the part of James's parable about dealing with obstructions to goal achievement. Romeo finds a circuitous way around the obstructions, the filings don't. Juliet's attractiveness can no more cause Romeo to get around an obstructing wall than the magnetic field can cause the filings to get around the obstructing card. In fact, Romeo will sometimes turn left and sometimes right in order to get to Juliet. A cause–effect explanation would mean that one cause (Juliet) has the ability to produce opposite effects (turning left or turning right) when necessary. That's a very unusual way for causes to behave.

Eventually, some scientific psychologists noticed that there were devices, called *control systems*, that seem to behave purposefully just like people. We met one of these devices in the previous chapter. A thermostat is a control system that appears to have the purpose of keeping the temperature in the house at some goal level. Not only that but, much like Romeo, the thermostat works around 'obstacles', like changes in outdoor temperature and the number of heat emitting people in the room, to achieve its goal. This convinced many psychologists that purposeful behavior was real and not just an illusion specific to the behavior of people (and other living things). But for psychologists who considered themselves scientific there was still the problem of the Law of Cause and Effect. Control systems are mechanical devices that have to obey the laws of physics even if their behavior seems to violate it. The solution was to admit that purposeful behavior was real but to assume that it could still be explained by cause and effect.

Control Theory as the Explanation of Purposeful Behavior

Psychologists developed many different theories aimed at explaining purposeful behavior in cause–effect terms. These theories were often very complex and highly mathematical but when you boiled them down to their essentials they all turned out to be versions of the 'magnet and iron filings' explanation of purposeful behavior. That is, they all assumed that some outside force, like the magnetic force exerted by the magnet, was responsible for the actions that achieved the goal. These theories appeared to work well enough in certain specific situations but they couldn't account for purposeful behavior as it was occurring in the real world. The problem turned out to be those pesky disturbances. While cause–effect theories could explain behavior that occurred when these disturbances weren't there — or when they came and went quickly — they failed when the disturbances were continuously changing. And the disturbances that occur in real life are generally changing all the time, such as the changing weight of the cup of coffee after each sip or the changing amount of push on the car by each wind gust.

Perhaps because they were trying to toe the strict cause–effect line, most psychologists missed the fact that the actual explanation of purposeful behavior had already been developed. The explanation is called *control theory* — the theory of how control systems do their controlling. It was left to William T. Powers to show that control theory was an explanation of *all* purposeful behavior — that of man-made control systems, such as thermostats, as well as that of living control systems — people. Powers was able to do this because he understood what we have described in this chapter — the fact that purposeful behavior *is a process of control.* So control theory is an explanation of virtually everything people do, from simple reflexes to writing books about control theory. The only exception is behavior that is not done on purpose — accidents such as falling off roofs and tripping on cracks — and even these can be understood as problems of control — failed control. The control theory explanation of behavior, which is described in the next chapters, is an explanation of the nature of controlling people. We see it as an explanation of the very nature of human nature.

Chapter 3

Perceptual Control Theory: How Purposeful Behavior Works

Understanding how things work may seem unimportant when those things are working as they should. But when things start to unravel or go off the rails, our ability to resolve the problem requires an understanding of what is causing it. When our car is working properly we don't care how it works but when it breaks down we call a mechanic to fix it because the mechanic knows how the car works. Similarly, when our teeth are working we don't care how they work but when we have a toothache we call a dentist to fix it because a dentist knows how teeth work. This applies to our own behavior as much as it does to our cars and teeth. When our behavior is working properly — when we are carrying out our purposes successfully so that we are 'in control' — knowing how behavior works may seem like it is only of academic interest. But when things start to go wrong — when we feel like we are losing control — we have to understand how our own behavior works so that we can fix it. And understanding how our behavior works means understanding how control works.

Control Theory

As noted in the previous chapter, controlling is a somewhat puzzling activity because it seems to violate the Law of Cause and Effect. A person who is controlling is taking actions in the present that appear to be caused by a goal that exists in the future. But if you have a thermostat in your house or cruise control in your car you know that the problem of how controlling works has been solved. Cruise control, for example, controls the speed of your car by bringing it to the 'cruising' speed you set as the goal, and keeps it there, protected from disturbances such as the changing inclination of the road. Engineers are able to build such devices — devices that control — because they have received the 'tablets' that explain how control works. On these 'tablets', which are actually engineering textbooks, is written *control theory*, which, despite its name, is not so much a theory as a description of the mechanism that makes all controlling possible, whether the controlling is done by a mechanical device, like the cruise control on your car, or a person. Since the controlling that people do is what we call their 'behavior', control theory provides an explanation of the behavior of controlling people.

Although the tablets describing control theory are not written in Hebrew, they are written in a language that many of us find difficult (or impossible) to understand: the language of advanced mathematics. But we believe you can get a good intuitive understanding of control theory — that is, of how controlling works — without having to learn to speak mathematics. As in the case of the Ten Commandments, where all you really have to know about them can be summed up as 'Do unto others as you would have them do unto you', all you really have to know about the mathematics of control theory can be summed up as: '*Behavior is the control of perception.*'[1] Control theory shows that the behavior of controlling people

— purposeful behavior — is a process of acting to keep our experience of the world — our perception — the way we want it to be. The rest, as they say, is commentary.

The Mechanism of Control

Things that control, be they gadgets or people, are called *control systems*. Control theory describes the mechanism that makes the controlling done by these control systems possible. The mechanism is made up of just three components: a *sensor*, a *comparator,* and an *effector.* The sensor (as its name implies) senses the current state of whatever it is that the control system controls — the controlled variable — and sends this information to the *comparator* as a signal called a *perception.* The sensor in your car's cruise control system is the speedometer which sends a perception of the car's speed, in the form of an electrical signal, to a comparator. The comparator measures the difference between the perception and a *reference signal,* which is a specification for the desired or goal state of that perception. The reference signal in the cruise control system is your setting of the desired cruise speed. Any difference between the perception and reference signal is an *error signal* that is converted by the effector into the actions of the control system. Note here that error does not mean 'bad', it just means 'different'. If a cruise control system is set to 50 mph, speeds of both 55 mph and 45 mph will be errors. In a cruise control system the effector converts the error signal into the rate at which the wheels are turning by adjusting the throttle position. The actions of the control system affect the controlled variable itself. The rate at which the wheels are turned affects the speed of the car.

And so we come full circle. The variable the system controls — the controlled variable — is linked, via the sensor, to the perception which is linked, via the comparator, to the error signal which is linked, via the effector, to actions that are linked back to the controlled variable. So the components of a control system are connected together in a *closed loop*. But just any closed loop won't do. There will only be control if the components of a control system are connected together to form a *negative feedback loop*. Negative feedback in control theory is not the same as the negative feedback your boss might give you about your presentation to the company directors. In a negative feedback loop, the 'negative' refers to the fact that the actions of a control system reduce (that is, have a negative effect on) the error that is the cause of those same actions. And having a negative effect on error is a positive thing because it means that the system is acting to bring the controlled variable close to the goal or reference state (since error is, after all, proportional to the difference between the perception of the state of the controlled variable and the reference signal that specifies the desired state of that perception). In cruise control systems, for example, the difference between actual and goal cruising speed — error — causes increases or decreases in wheel turning speed — actions — that bring cruising speed — the controlled variable — closer to the goal speed, thus reducing the error that caused those actions. By acting to reduce the error that causes its actions, a negative feedback loop brings a controlled variable to the reference or goal state and keeps it there protected from disturbances that would increase the error. So when a negative feedback loop is acting to reduce its own error, it is controlling. The negative feedback relationship between the components of a control system is the mechanism of control.

We should mention that the other way the components of a closed-loop can be connected is called a *positive feedback loop*. Just as 'negative' means 'good' in a negative feedback loop, 'positive' means 'bad' in a positive feedback loop. In a positive feedback loop the actions of the system increase (that is, have a positive effect on) the cause of those same actions. The most familiar (and annoying) example of a positive feedback loop is probably the audio feedback from a microphone. This is a situation where the audio output of the loop — the sound coming out of the speakers — amplifies rather than cancels the cause of that output — the sound going into the microphone — leading to a runaway situation where the output quickly gets extremely loud. There is no controlled variable in a positive feedback loop because there is no control. The sound in the audio feedback loop isn't brought to a goal state; rather it just keeps getting louder until someone moves the mike or the circuit blows.

Control of Perception

Perhaps the most surprising thing we learn from a control theory analysis of how control systems work is that a negative feedback loop controls a perception of the controlled variable, not the controlled variable itself. The cruise control system, for example, controls a perception of the car's speed in the form of the speedometer's measure of speed, not the actual speed itself. We know that a control system controls a perception because the error that is reduced by the negative feedback loop is the difference between the reference signal and perception of the controlled variable. When the negative feedback loop acts to reduce error it is making a perception of the controlled variable match the reference signal. So in the cruise control system, when you set the reference signal for cruising speed to 65 mph, the cruise control makes a perception of the car's speed match that reference speed.

Engineers who build control systems have to be aware of the fact that these systems control perceptions because it means that the sensors must provide an accurate measure (an accurate perception) of the variable to be controlled in order for the system to work properly. A properly functioning control system is one that brings the controlled variable to the reference signal setting. For example, a properly functioning thermostat is one that brings the room temperature to 68°F when you set the reference temperature to 68°F. But this will only happen if the sensor in the thermostat provides an accurate perception of the actual room temperature. If, for example, the sensor is 'off' so that it provides a perception of temperature that is only 80% of the actual temperature then the control system will not think that the room temperature is at the reference of 68°F until the actual room temperature is 85°F. Of course, if you had such a thermostat you could compensate for this problem by learning to set the reference temperature to something like 54°F to get the room to a comfortable temperature. But a better solution would be to buy a more accurate thermostat.

It is particularly important to know that control systems control their perceptions when these systems happen to be people rather than gadgets such as thermostats. It is important because it means that in order to understand people's behavior — what they are doing — we have to learn what perceptions they are trying to control. This is because when we look at people's behavior we are looking at controlling from the outside, so to speak. That is, the behavior we see — our 'outside' view of a person's behavior — is just the means that the person uses to maintain perceptions in reference states — the person's 'inside' view of their own behavior. For example, when we watch a person typing at a computer, our outside view is that of a person moving their fingers and hands to different locations on the keyboard; but their inside view is of perceiving the desired letters appearing on the computer screen. Control theory shows it is impossible to correctly understand the outside view of a person's behavior without knowing the inside view. That is, in order to understand a person's behavior — the typing movement, for example — we have to know what perceptions the person is controlling — which letters the typist wants to see appearing on the screen. So control theory points to the importance of understanding a person's behavior in terms of the perceptions the person is controlling. Because of this, when control theory is applied to understanding human behavior it has come to be called *Perceptual Control Theory* or *PCT*.

What Are You Doing?

So PCT is control theory applied to understanding the behavior of controlling people. Whereas most psychological theories attempt to explain behavior from an outside observer's perspective, PCT is unique inasmuch as it is an explanation of behavior from the perspective of the person doing the behaving. One way to state the basic lesson of PCT is that we can't understand what people are doing by just looking at what they are doing. Of course, we are using the term 'doing' here to mean two different things. 'Doing' can refer to a person's actions as well as the purpose of those actions (what the person wants to perceive). So what we are saying here is that you can't tell the purpose of people's behavior by just looking at their actions. You may have experienced this phenomenon yourself if you have ever seen someone doing something and asked yourself 'what are they doing'? Since you can clearly see the person's behavior (their actions), what you must be asking yourself about is the purpose of those actions. Why, for example, is the person gesticulating like that? Are they speaking to someone in sign language, hailing a cab, waving to a friend? What is the person's purpose?

The fact that this happens — that we find ourselves wondering what people are doing even though we can see perfectly well what they are doing — suggests that we often understand, at least intuitively, what PCT tells us, which is that there is more to behavior than meets the eye. From a PCT perspective, in order to know what a person is doing — what the purpose of their behavior is — we have to know what perception they are controlling. In the case of the person gesticulating, for example, the possible purposes of this behavior may be to control a perception of talking in sign language, hailing a cab, or waving to a friend. Since we can't see another person's perceptions, however, we can't really tell what a person's purpose is by just looking at their behavior.

So we should never assume that we can tell what people are doing — what their purposes are — by just looking at what they are doing — their behavior. But more often than not we do make this assumption. Apparently this results from our human propensity to see behavior in terms of purpose. This was first demonstrated in a classic experiment in social psychology done by Fritz Heider and Marianne Simmel[2]. Heider and Simmel showed that people will see purpose in behavior even if that behavior is not actually purposeful. They demonstrated this by having people describe the behavior of objects moving around in an animated film[*]. The objects — two triangles and a circle — moved in and out of a large rectangle, sometimes together and sometimes alone, in rather complicated patterns. So the objects were not moving around randomly but they were not control systems so their behavior really had no purpose. But people observing this behavior would attribute purpose to it; sometimes very elaborate purposes. For example, many people saw one

---

[*] *https://youtu.be/n9TWwG4SFWQ.*

triangle as trying to abduct the circle while the other triangle was trying to save it.

Apparently, people can't help seeing behavior as purposeful, even when it's not. The inclination to see purpose in the behavior of inanimate objects (like those in the Heider-Simmel film) is called 'animism'. Our animistic inclinations show up when we curse the wind for blowing dust in our eyes (as though the wind had the purpose of blinding us) or protest at the rain for ruining the shine on our newly washed car (as though the rain had the purpose of ruining the appearance of our car). So our animistic tendencies often lead us to see purpose in activity that has no purpose. But they also lead us to jump to conclusions about the purpose of behavior that actually is purposeful, conclusions that can be quite incorrect. This happens so often in literature that it is hard to choose the best example but surely some of the most amusing ones occur in Jane Austen's *Emma* in which the title character sees nearly everything her friends do as evidence of their having a romantic interest in the people Emma thinks they should be attached to. *Emma* is actually the story of the world champion at jumping to the wrong conclusions about people's purposes.

Mind Reading

Although our conclusions about the purpose of a person's behavior are often wrong, they are also often right. The problem is that we are not very good at telling the difference. If, for example, we conclude that the gesticulating person is signing to a deaf friend we may be right and we may be wrong. The trouble is we often act on our conclusions as though they are right whether or not they are actually right. But sometimes we are able to test our conclusion by getting more information. For example, we can test our conclusion about the purpose of the gesticulating by looking to see if the person who seems to be the deaf friend signs back. If not, then it is evidence that our conclusion was wrong; the purpose of the gesticulating is not signing to a deaf friend. If we are really interested in figuring out what the person's purpose is then we might come up with another hypothesis about the purpose of the gesticulating. Our next hypothesis might be that the gesticulating person is hailing a cab. So we wait to see if a cab pulls up. If it does, then we can be pretty sure that the purpose of the gesticulating was to hail a cab. If not, then we might try another hypothesis.

This approach to testing our conclusions about the purpose of behavior is actually very similar to a formal approach to understanding purposeful behavior known as 'The Test for the Controlled Variable' or simply *The Test*. Recall that, according to PCT, understanding behavior requires knowing what is going on inside the person doing the behaving. And what is going on inside the person is that perceptions are being controlled. These perceptions are the controlled variables that The Test is testing for. When you know what perception a person is controlling you know the purpose of their behavior. But perceptions are private; they exist only in the mind (or brain, if you prefer) of the person controlling them. Finding out what perception a person is controlling would seem to require the ability to read minds. And, indeed, The Test lets us do something very much like mind reading, though it involves perfectly natural methods — nothing supernatural is involved.

The Test is based on the basic PCT principle that a negative feedback loop will act to resist disturbances that would otherwise push a controlled perception away from its specified reference state. This principle is based on the fact that a negative feedback loop hates error and is continuously acting to get rid of it. Disturbances are effects on controlled perceptions that increase error so the effects of these disturbances are immediately opposed. This means that we can 'read' whether or not a perception is controlled by seeing whether or not disturbances to that perception are opposed. In order to do this we have to start with a hypothesis about the perception that is being controlled. In the case of our gesticulating person, our starting hypothesis was that the person was trying to perceive talking in sign language to a deaf friend. Next we have to think of things that would be disturbances to this variable. If the gesticulating person is controlling a perception of talking to a deaf friend then a disturbance would be the presence or absence of someone signing back. If there is someone signing back then that would create an error in our gesticulating person that would be opposed by signing in reply. If there is no one signing back then this would also create an error that would be opposed by the gesticulating person no longer signing.

The next step in The Test is to see if the disturbance to the hypothetical controlled perception is opposed as expected. If it is, it is evidence that the assumed perception is under control. If not, it is evidence that the perception is not under control and the next step is to start over with a new hypothesis about what the perception is that is being controlled. This is what was done in the case of the gesticulating person. Since there was no opposition to the disturbance of having no one signing back — the gesticulating didn't stop as expected — a new hypothesis about the controlled perception was proposed — the perception of hailing a cab. Once the new hypothesis about the controlled perception is proposed, The Test proceeds as before, looking to see whether disturbances to that variable are, in fact, opposed. This process continues until you are convinced that all disturbances to the perception you think is under control are opposed.

This is a description of a rather informal way of doing The Test. The actual, formal version of The Test is much more precise and can provide a startlingly accurate picture of what is inside another person's mind — what perception they are controlling — even when this is not at all obvious from watching their 'outside' behavior. The accuracy of a formal version of the test is illustrated in an interactive internet demonstration that we call the 'Mind Reading' game[*]. In this game you are asked to move any one of three avatars around the screen using the mouse controller. The game is set up so that when you move one avatar you are actually moving all three. So your 'outside' behavior — the behavior an observer can see — is the movements of the three avatars and the movements of the mouse. But your inside behavior is your perception of the one avatar you are moving 'on purpose'. The game is set up this way so that it is impossible to tell which of the three avatars is being moved 'on purpose' by simply looking at the movements of the avatars. All three avatars are moving around the screen and there is nothing about the movement of the purposefully moved avatar that distinguishes it from the others that are being moved 'accidentally'. So this is a situation where an observer cannot tell what you are doing (which avatar you are moving on purpose) by just observing what you are doing (observing the movements of the avatars or the mouse).

The only way to know what you are doing in this game is by determining what perception you are controlling, which in this case means determining which avatar you are moving around the screen on purpose. That is, the only way to tell what you are doing — what you are controlling — is by

---

[*] *http://www.mindreadings.com/ControlDemo/Mindread.html.*

reading your mind. The computer does this mind reading using The Test. The computer is simultaneously testing three hypotheses about the perception you are controlling — each hypothesis corresponding to the perception of a different one of the three avatars. It turns out that each avatar is being pushed around by different disturbances. So the computer can 'read your mind' by determining which of the three disturbances is being most consistently opposed by your actions (the mouse movements). Once the computer has detected the avatar that is being moved on purpose it lets you know by changing the avatar into a new person. At that point you can 'change your mind' and start moving a different avatar on purpose and the computer will soon determine the avatar that you are now controlling. This game works best when you are able to control the position of the avatars rather skillfully. But once you have learned to do this we think you may find it surprising — and possibly even enjoyable — to see how The Test can detect what's on your mind, even when you are changing your mind.

It is the Cause, My Reference Signal

The 'Mind Reading' game is worth getting to know because it demonstrates two important principles of PCT at the same time. One we have just discussed: the principle of *disturbance resistance* and how it can be used to determine the purpose of behavior. The second could be called the principle of *autonomy*. This refers to the fact that human control systems set their own reference signals for the perceptions they control. This is quite different than the way reference signals are set in human-made control systems like the thermostat, where they are set by someone outside the system. In the Mind Reading game the autonomous setting of a reference signal is seen in the changing position of the purposefully moved avatar. The changing position of this avatar reflects the changing setting of your reference signal specifying its desired position.

What you are doing autonomously when you set a reference signal in your brain is similar to what you would be doing when you set the reference signal for a mechanical device such as a cruise control system. You are varying the setting of the reference signal in your brain for the position of the avatar in the same way you would vary the setting of the reference signal for cruising speed. If you continuously vary the reference signal for cruising speed, increasing and decreasing it slowly, the speed of the car will increase and decrease right along with it, though at a slight delay. The same thing is happening when you vary the reference signal in your brain for the position of an avatar in the Mind Reading game. As you vary the reference signal for the position of the avatar the position of the avatar varies right along with it, also at a slight delay.

So changing the reference signal of a control system, whether the reference is set from outside the system (as in the cruise control system) or inside it (as in people), results in corresponding changes in the variable that is being controlled. This happens because changes in the reference signal result in errors — discrepancies between the reference signal and the perception of the controlled variable — which are eliminated by the actions of the negative feedback loop. So the error reducing mechanism of the negative feedback loop keeps the perception of the controlled variable matching the reference signal, even if the reference signal is changing continuously. Indeed, the negative feedback loop is doing 'double duty' when the reference signal is changing because it is still acting to resist disturbances to the controlled variable. So the negative feedback loop of the cruise control system is continuously bringing the perceived speed of the car into a match with your changes in the setting of the reference signal for cruising speed while, at the same time, compensating for disturbances such as changes in the inclination of the road. The same thing is happening when you autonomously vary the setting of your reference signal for the position of an avatar in the Mind Reading game. The negative feedback loop of your 'avatar control system' is continuously bringing the perceived position of the avatar into a match with your autonomously produced changes in the setting of the reference signal for the position of the avatar while, at the same time, compensating for disturbances to the position of the avatar — the pushes and pulls on the avatar that are being produced by the computer.

If we think of the purposefully produced states of perceptions, such as the perception of the position of a car or the position of an avatar on the screen, as what the person is 'doing' — their behavior — then the ultimate cause of a person's behavior is the setting of reference signals in the brain. This is what is going on in the Mind Reading game when you are purposefully moving one of the avatars around the screen. Although all the avatars are moving around the screen when you move the mouse, the movement of only one of the avatars is a purposefully varied perception. The purposely produced movement of the avatar is caused by autonomous variations in the setting of the reference signal specifying the desired position of that avatar. The reference signal causes the desired variations in the position of the controlled avatar via the operation of the negative feedback loop. But the ultimate cause of the behavior of the avatar is variations in the reference signal. So the ultimate cause of the behavior of the purposefully moved avatar — your behavior — is you, in the person of your autonomously set reference signals.

A Behavioral Illusion

The idea that we are the cause of our own behavior seems to be contradicted by the fact that our behavior often seems to be caused by external events. A familiar example is the patellar or 'knee jerk' reflex where a behavior, the 'knee jerk', appears to be caused by an external event, the tap of a rubber hammer just below the kneecap. There are many other reflexes like this, where we don't seem to be the cause of our own behavior. For example, there is the eye blink reflex where a blink (the behavior) appears to be caused by air puffed at the eye (the external event), and the pupillary reflex where changes in the size of the pupil (the behavior) appear to be caused by changes in the amount of light shined at the eye (the external event). Indeed, experimental studies in psychology are done with the goal of finding the external events (called independent variables) that are the cause of various behaviors (called dependent variables). So we find experiments that appear to show that viewing an aggressive model causes aggressive behavior or that the demands of an authority figure cause compliant behavior.

So what's going on here? Can behavior be both autonomous and driven by external events? PCT shows us that the answer is a qualified 'yes'. The answer is 'yes' because once we have autonomously selected the reference setting for a controlled variable we will have to act in a way that opposes the effect of disturbances that would push that variable away from the reference state. For example, once you have decided to keep the cursor on target in a tracking task, your actions (mouse movements) must precisely oppose disturbances that would push the cursor from the target. Or suppose your friend wanted to show you a new hiking trail she had found and you decided to travel to the start of the trail in separate cars. In order to avoid getting lost, you decide to keep your car approximately 30ft behind your friend's car. Once you have autonomously established this goal of the distance you want to be behind your friend's car, your friend is then able to control the speed at which you drive. If your friend accelerates, you will have to accelerate, if your friend brakes, you will have to brake. At least, you will have to do these things if you wish to maintain the goal of staying a specified distance behind your friend. So outside events — disturbances to the perceptions you control — will appear to be causing your behavior — the actions that compensate for the effects of these disturbances. In this way, your behavior is both autonomous and driven by external events. You have autonomously selected the purpose of your behavior — keeping the cursor on target, staying a fixed distance behind your friend's car — while the behavior used to achieve this purpose — the movement of the mouse, accelerating and braking the car — is driven by external events — the disturbances.

The qualification to the idea that the behavior of a control system can be both autonomous and driven by external events is that the external events that drive behavior are not actually the cause of that behavior. Recall from our analysis of a negative feedback loop that the actual cause of the actions that compensate for disturbances is error — the discrepancy between perception and reference — not the disturbances themselves. So the apparent causal connection between external events (disturbances) and the behavior of a control system is something of an illusion. Powers called it 'the behavioral illusion'[3]. The illusion is that disturbances are a direct cause of a person's actions when, in fact, those actions are caused by error. And error is caused by both the effect of disturbances on a controlled perception and the setting of the reference signal for that perception. This means that the same external event will have different effects on behavior (or no effect at all) depending on the setting of the reference for the controlled perception.

What this all comes down to is that our autonomy can 'override' the effect of external events on our behavior. For example, we will typically dodge when someone feints punching us in the face. An external event — the punch moving toward our face — appears to cause our behavior — the dodge. But PCT tells us that we dodge because the punch is a disturbance to a controlled perception — the perception of the pain that would result if the punch landed. We dodge the punch because our reference for pain is apparently set at zero. But we can prevent the punch from causing us to dodge — that is, we can override the effect of an external event on our behavior — by resetting our reference signal for pain to a value much greater than zero, which is what someone might be willing to do who wanted to appear to be tough (or non-violent).

So PCT shows us that the effect of external events on the behavior of controlling people actually depends on their autonomy. External events cause actions only when those events are disturbances to a controlled variable. Because we autonomously specify the setting of the reference signals that specify the desired values of the perceptual variables we control, we determine whether or not an external event will be a disturbance that requires compensating action. What we haven't explored yet is how this autonomy is implemented. That is, we still need to know what it is inside of us that is setting — and resetting — our reference signals. What, for example, changes the setting of our reference signal for pain from zero to a value greater than zero? This will be the subject of the next chapter.

Chapter 4

We Contain Multitudes

People are not just one big control system controlling one perception relative to one reference signal. To paraphrase Walt Whitman,[1] we contain multitudes of control systems. In fact, we *are* multitudes of control systems. And all of these control systems are operating at the same time. This means that we are controlling lots of different perceptions simultaneously. For example, we can control our perception of walking while we control our perception of chewing gum while we control our perception of putting in their place the person who says we can't do both at the same time. Moreover, the multitudes of control systems that make up a controlling person seem to be arranged in a hierarchy where the systems at the lower levels are used as the means of achieving the goals of systems at the higher levels. There are several very compelling pieces of evidence that this is the case.

Hierarchical Control

One piece of evidence for a hierarchy of control systems is behavioral. Almost anything people do can be seen as a process of accomplishing a hierarchy of purposes or goals. Typing these words into the computer is a good example. The highest level goal is getting the words typed, which is accomplished by achieving the lower level goal of getting my fingers to the right keys which is accomplished by achieving the still lower level goal of producing the muscle forces that move my hands and fingers properly. Actually, getting these words typed is a lower level means of achieving the higher level goal of getting this book written, which is a means of achieving an even higher level goal of helping people understand PCT. So there are many levels of goal achievement involved in even an apparently simple behavior such as typing words into a computer.

All these goals are being accomplished at the same time, with the accomplishment of the lower level goals nested within the accomplishment of the higher level ones. That is, I am achieving my muscle contraction goals while I am achieving my finger position goals while I am achieving my word typing goals, and so on.

Another piece of evidence is neurophysiological. The brain and spinal cord — the central nervous system (CNS) — seem to consist of a hierarchical arrangement of neural structures that could implement a hierarchical arrangement of control systems. The lowest level structures in the CNS are the sensory-motor neural connections in the spinal cord. These are the structures that implement the spinal reflexes that are involved in achieving low level behavioral goals, such as the goal of producing particular muscle forces. Above these sits the brain stem which contains structures that are involved in achieving more complex goals, such as the goal of producing the particular configuration of muscle forces that results in a clenched fist. This hierarchical arrangement of neural structures continues up from the brain stem to the cerebellum, which contains structures that are involved in achieving even more complex goals, such as the goal of producing the sequence of hand configurations that is seen as grasping and releasing a pen. The top of the hierarchical arrangement of the CNS is the cerebral cortex, which is involved in achieving the most complex goals people can achieve, such as solving math problems, writing symphonies, and creating world peace.

The Theory of Relative Autonomy

These and other pieces of evidence are consistent with the idea that the multitudes of control systems that make up a controlling person are arranged in a hierarchy. Such a hierarchical arrangement provides a nice explanation of how we are able to set our own references (goals) for the perceptions we control. PCT assumes that reference signal specifications for the perceptions controlled by control systems at a particular level in your hierarchy of control systems are set by control systems at a higher level in that hierarchy. For example, when you are typing words into a computer the constantly changing reference specifications for the perception of the key you are pressing is provided by a higher level control system, probably the one that is controlling the perception of the words you want typed. So the 'you' that sets your references (goals) for what you want to perceive is another higher level control system inside of you.

The higher level control system that sets the goals of a lower level control system doesn't do this setting arbitrarily. This was implied in the example of typing a word where the lower level system's goals for the keys to be pressed depend on the word that the higher level system wants typed. If the higher level system wants to perceive the word 'control' typed then it has to tell the lower level system to first type a 'c' then 'o' and so on. That is, the control system that is the higher level you — the you that wants to type 'control' — has to set the goal of typing 'c' and then 'o' and so on for the system that is the lower level you in order to get the word 'control' typed. So the control systems in a hierarchy are not free to set goals in any way they want. The goals that are set for lower level perceptions are always constrained by the goals of the higher level systems that set those goals.

So our *autonomy* — the freedom we have to set our own goals and thus carry out our own purposes — can be seen as being relative. The goals set for lower level control systems are set relative to the goals of higher level systems that 'use' these lower level systems as the means to achieve their own goals. So once a goal, such as perceiving your car staying in its lane, has been selected by a higher level system, the goals that can be selected for the lower level system, the one that sets the goal for turning the steering wheel, are now constrained to be only those that achieve the higher level goal. In this case you are constrained to selecting only those goals for the steering wheel position that will keep the car in its lane.

This *relativity of autonomy* applies all the way up the hierarchy of control systems. You can only select lower level goals that achieve higher level ones. The goals that are set for the very lowest level control systems in the hierarchy are constrained to be those that will achieve the goals of the systems at the next level up that are setting these goals. And the same applies to those systems at the next level up, and the next level up after that, and so on.

If you think of autonomy as freedom to do whatever you want then the relative autonomy of a control system hierarchy may not seem to be very autonomous. And you would be right. The control systems in a control hierarchy are only relatively free. They are free to set goals for other control systems, but only those goals that will achieve the goals of the higher level systems that are setting those goals. So once you have decided to go to the store (the higher level goal), the only routes you can take (the lower level goals), are those that will get you there. So your higher level goals limit your freedom to 'do what you want' in terms of selecting your lower order goals.

While seeing ourselves as a hierarchy of control systems doesn't mean we are autonomous in the sense of being free to do whatever we want, it does mean we are autonomous in the sense that we do set our own goals. Unlike mechanical control systems, like the thermostat, our goals cannot be set from outside us. Our goals — the reference signals that specify what should happen — can only be set by other control systems inside us. No one else can set our goals for us and we cannot set theirs. This is a painful fact that is known only too well by parents who want their children to keep their rooms tidy, or to arrive home at a certain time, or to study particular degrees at university, or to make friends only with particular people. The goal setting done by human controllers is a completely private, personal affair. Telling people what goals to have is not the same as setting the temperature goal for a thermostat. The difference, of course, is that you directly affect the reference signal (goal) setting of the thermostat while you have no direct access to the reference signal setting of a person. Telling someone to have a particular goal is just a disturbance to some perception the person is controlling. For example, if you tell a person to make a right turn you are asking them to have the goal of perceiving themselves turning right. This will not necessarily lead to the person adopting this goal, particularly if the person has the goal of continuing straight ahead. In that case your request will be a disturbance to the perception of continuing on a straight course and is more likely to be met with an irritated glare or a plea that you stop being a backseat driver than a change of goals. So while we are only relatively autonomous in terms of how free we are to set our own goals, we are absolutely autonomous in terms of the fact that we are the only ones who can set our own goals.

A Hierarchy of Skill

The hierarchy of control systems is the PCT explanation of how we are able to carry out skilled behaviors — from simple behaviors, such as pressing a key on a keyboard, to complex ones, such as writing a book. Since, according to PCT, behavior is the control of perception, simple skilled behaviors involve the control of simple perceptions while more complex behaviors involve the control of more complex perceptions. Pressing a key involves the control of a simpler perception than writing a sentence. PCT assumes control systems low in the hierarchy control perceptions that are less complex than those controlled by the control systems that are higher up. So pressing a key is carried out by a lower level control system while writing a sentence is carried out by a higher level one.

Skilled behavior, then, is the result of the operation of a hierarchy of control systems that control perceptions that increase in complexity as you move up the hierarchy. Moreover, the control systems higher up in the hierarchy control their perceptions by setting the reference signals (goals) for the perceptions controlled by systems at the lower level. So the higher level system controlling for the perception of a sentence — a very complex perception — controls for this perception by specifying the goals for perceptions controlled by systems at lower levels — such as those controlling for perceptions of words, letters, and key presses. In order to write a sentence, the system controlling for the perception of the sentence would have to keep changing the goals of the lower level systems controlling for the perception of words, which would have to keep changing the goals for the still lower level systems controlling for the perception of letters, which would have to keep changing the goals for the still lower level systems controlling for the perception of a particular key being pressed. All these control systems would be acting at the same time so that the lowest level perceptions — the key presses — are being controlled at the same time as the highest level one — the sentence.

We call the behavior produced by the control hierarchy *skilled* because you had to learn how to do it. That is, you had to learn how to vary the actions of the control systems so that they can bring perceptions to the specified states while compensating for disturbances that would prevent this from happening. You even had to learn *which* lower level perceptions to control in order to control the highest level perceptions. For example, in order to skillfully type a sentence, you first had to learn to perceive a sentence. Then you had to learn how to vary the goals for the lower level control systems — the one's controlling for perceptions of words, letters, and key presses — in order to produce the sentence you want to perceive. What you are doing is building a well-oiled control hierarchy that allows you to produce skilled behaviors like typing sentences.

The behaviors produced by the control hierarchy are also skilled in the sense that they can be carried out unconsciously — not that they always are, but they can be. Much of your skilled controlling occurs outside of consciousness. For example, we are usually unconscious of the fact that we are controlling our balance or the keys we are pressing to type words. So the control hierarchy can be considered the automatic, mechanical part of us. It's the 'machine' that allows us to carry out our purposes (once we have tuned it properly) but there is, indeed, a ghost in it. The ghost of 'consciousness'. It's not a scary ghost. Indeed, it's a very helpful ghost. We will discuss the important role of this *ghost in the machine* in the next chapter.

It's Turtles All the Way Up

You may have noticed that there is a bit of a problem if the multitudes of control systems that we contain are arranged in a hierarchy. The problem is this: If the goals of control systems at each level of a control hierarchy are set by the systems above them, then what sets the goals of those systems at the very top of the hierarchy? The problem is similar to the one confronted by people who believe that the world is a flat plate supported on the back of a giant turtle. One such person, when asked what the turtle was standing on, is said to have replied 'It's turtles all the way down!'.[2] In the case of the control hierarchy we could answer the question of what sets the goals of the systems at the top of the hierarchy by saying 'it's turtles all the way up'. But we know that there must be a top to the hierarchy because nature abhors an infinite regress and also because the hierarchy is implemented in our nervous system, which does have a top, the cerebral cortex.

The problem with having a top to a hierarchy of control systems is that there is nothing above it that can set the goals of the control systems. Those systems, therefore, are like thermostats whose temperature is set at the factory to a particular temperature and nothing can change them. So autonomy, at least of the relative kind, seems to end at the top of the hierarchy of control systems. It would seem that we can't change our highest level goals because there is no higher level reason to change them.

It has been suggested that our highest level goals concern very complex perceptions, such as the perceptions of the kind of person we are — whether we perceive ourselves as a liberal or conservative, Christian or Jew, Yankee or Red Sox fan, and so on. And it does seem that people rarely do change their goals about the kind of person they perceive themselves to be. Yankee fans rarely become Red Sox fans, and vice versa. But it does happen. And according to PCT it happens as a result of the operation of that ghost in the machine that we mentioned earlier. Consciousness seems to be in charge in some way of making fundamental changes to the control hierarchy when such changes seem needed. And changing one's goals about what kind of person one wants to be is a very fundamental change to one's control hierarchy. The next chapter is about why such changes are sometimes necessary and how they are made.

Chapter 5

Zen and the Art of Controlling

We can see the control hierarchy as the 'motorcycle' of the mind, driving purposeful behavior by controlling a hierarchy of perceptions. And like a real motorcycle, the motorcycle of the mind needs constant maintenance.[1] According to PCT this maintenance is done by something called the *reorganization system*. The reorganization system is called that because it reorganizes parts of the control hierarchy when things go wrong. We'll discuss some of the important reasons why things go wrong in a later chapter. For now, we will just note that things do go wrong with the control hierarchy for various reasons. What 'going wrong' means in this case is that one or more of the perceptions controlled by control systems in the hierarchy are not being kept in their reference or goal state. In other words, control of one or more perceptions is lost. For example, if your relationship with your partner is not what you want it to be, then you have lost control of this relationship; you are not keeping your perception of the relationship in its goal state.

When you lose control there is a discrepancy between what you want (your goal) and what you are getting (what you perceive) that you are not able to correct. In the case of a relationship there is a discrepancy between the good relationship you want and the not so good relationship that you are currently experiencing and, for some reason, you can't bridge that gap. As you may recall, this discrepancy is called error and in a properly functioning negative feedback loop, this error would cause actions that reduce that error. But when something goes wrong in the control hierarchy, the negative feedback loop no longer works properly, and the error persists. Persistent error in a control hierarchy is like the constant noise made by a malfunctioning motorcycle — it is very unpleasant and we want it to go away. Usually we try the things that have worked in the past to reduce error but, sometimes, error persists despite our best efforts to remove it. We experience persistent error in the form of stress, anxiety, depression, or some other type of misery, madness, or psychological distress. The job of the reorganization system is to get rid of persistent error in the control hierarchy.

Walk Like a Bacterium

Unlike a motorcycle mechanic, the reorganization system doesn't actually know what to do to fix the control hierarchy when things go wrong. That's because the reorganization system isn't very smart. All it can do is determine whether or not things are going wrong — it can 'feel' the error — and it can fiddle with the components of the control systems in the hierarchy. But it turns out this is all the reorganization system needs to be able to do to fix things up when they go wrong. Although the reorganization system doesn't know exactly what to do to make things better, it can see whether or not what it is doing is working because it can monitor the error in the control hierarchy and determine if it is decreasing or not.

The way the reorganization system fixes the control hierarchy is similar to the way the E. coli bacterium navigates to food. The problem for E. coli is similar to that of the reorganization system. The bacterium doesn't know what movements to make in order to get to the food any more than the reorganization system knows what changes to make to fix persistent error in a control system. This is because E. coli can't just direct itself toward the food and head off over to it. The bacterium can only move in a straight line from whatever direction it is facing, or it can stop moving and 'tumble' until it is facing a new direction, and then start moving again in another straight line. The new direction after a tumble is randomly related to the direction before the tumble. So E. coli can't actively steer towards the food, but it can tell whether it is moving toward or away from the food because it can sense a change in the concentration of the chemical nutrients surrounding the food. If E. coli is moving toward the food the sensed concentration of nutrients will increase, otherwise the sensed concentration will stay the same or decrease. So, just as the reorganization system can tell whether or not what it is doing is reducing error in the control hierarchy, E. coli can tell whether or not the direction in which it is moving is getting it closer to the food.

E. coli is able to navigate to the food even though it can only randomly select the direction in which it is moving because it spends more time moving in the right direction than in the wrong one. When E. coli senses that it is moving in the wrong direction it quickly stops, tumbles around briefly, and sets off in a new, randomly selected direction. If E. coli senses that this new direction is moving it towards the food (it senses that the nutrient concentration is increasing), it will wait longer before tumbling again than it would if it sensed that it was moving away from the food. So E. coli is able to navigate to food without knowing how to get there using a biased random trial and error process. The bias is to spend more time going in the right than in the wrong randomly selected direction. This process turns out to be quite effective — almost as effective as turning and steering directly toward the food. You can see this biased random walk process in action in a demonstration available on the internet.[2]

According to PCT, the reorganization system fixes persistent error in your control hierarchy using the same biased random walk process as E. coli uses to navigate to food. It uses this process because, like E. coli, the reorganization system doesn't know what to do to reach its goal, which is to eliminate persistent error in the control hierarchy — to get rid of the irritating noise made by the motorcycle. If the reorganization system knew what to do to eliminate persistent error when it pops up in the control hierarchy we would never have any problems; or at least we wouldn't have them for very long. The 'motorcycle' of our mind would always be running nearly perfectly. But we do have problems with our 'motorcycle' — our control hierarchy — and we feel the error associated with those problems as psychological distress. We typically go about trying to solve those problems in a somewhat random, trial and error way. We believe the 'we' that is doing this is our reorganization system. The random trial and error things we do to try to solve our problems are analogous to the random changes in E. coli's direction after each tumble. The random things we do to feel better are the random 'fiddling' of the reorganization system with the components of the control systems that make up the control hierarchy. Fiddling with the sensor of a control system results in perceiving things in a new way. Fiddling with the comparator results in a new way of creating error. And fiddling with the effector results in new ways of setting goals for lower level control systems.

While the fiddling done by the reorganization system is completely random, the results of this fiddling can be sensed in the form of an increase or decrease in the overall error in the control hierarchy — in one's level of psychological distress. So the reorganization system can tell whether or not its fiddling is making things better. And we assume that the reorganization system can bias its random fiddling to reach its goal of reducing error in the same way that E. coli biases its random walk to reach its goal of getting to food. The reorganization system does it by increasing the time between 'fiddles' when the result of a fiddle is a reduction in error and reducing the time between fiddles when the result of a fiddle is an increase in error.

The biased random walk approach to reaching a goal can be effective and efficient. But it is not guaranteed to reach the goal in a timely manner. This is especially true when there are a lot of 'moving parts' that all have to be working properly in order for a goal to be achieved. In the case of the E. coli bacterium there was only one 'moving part' (literally) involved in getting to the goal: the direction of movement of the bacterium. But there are often many moving parts involved in achieving the reorganization system's goal of reducing error in the control hierarchy of humans. These are the components of the many control systems that are no longer working properly and are, therefore, contributing to the amount of error — psychological distress — sensed by the reorganization system. With so many moving parts involved, even a biased random walk approach to achieving a goal could take forever, which is effectively a failure since we don't have forever to wait for a solution to our control problems.

Consciousness and Reorganization

It would help things enormously, in terms of the efficiency of the control hierarchy repair process, if the reorganization system could at least direct its random fiddling to the control system or systems in the control hierarchy that are the actual cause of the problem. Like the mechanic who knows whether the problem with the motorcycle is in the engine, transmission, or brakes, it would be nice if the reorganization system could determine whether the problem with the control hierarchy was in the system controlling for keeping your balance, eating dessert, or maintaining a good relationship with your spouse. That is, it would be nice if the reorganization system included a mechanism that makes it possible to identify the systems in the control hierarchy that might be causing the psychological distress and didn't alter any systems that were already working. We believe that such a mechanism does exist and it exists in the form of consciousness.

Consciousness is a rather mysterious phenomenon because it is completely private. Unlike behavior, we can't experience the consciousness of other people; we can only experience our own. But one thing we can learn from examining our own consciousness is that it is clearly separate from the control hierarchy. We can clearly control — that is, we can carry out our purposes — unconsciously. This is an important observation because consciousness is often assumed to be a necessary prerequisite for carrying out one's purposes. But, in fact, we carry out most of our purposes completely unconsciously. For example, you may have had the experience of becoming 'lost in thought' while driving down the highway. During this time you were not consciously carrying out many purposes, such as keeping the car in its lane, maintaining its speed, and avoiding collisions with other cars. That is, you were not consciously controlling your perception of the position of the car in its lane, the speed of the car, or the distance of your car from other cars. But you were controlling these things — you were carrying out these purposes unconsciously — or your car would have ended up in a terrible collision a few seconds after you became unconscious of them. Another rather dramatic example of carrying out purposes (controlling) unconsciously is sleep-walking. People who walk in their sleep are apparently completely unconscious of the fact that they are carrying out some rather complex purposes while they are asleep. For example, if you have ever gone to sleep in one room and woken up in another with no knowledge of ever having walked from one room to the other, you know that you were able to do some rather complex controlling — maintaining your balance while avoiding obstacles — in order to get from one place to another successfully, with no consciousness of having done this at all.

Not only can we carry out our purposes unconsciously but consciousness can move around so as to make us aware of carrying out purposes of which we were previously unaware. In the driving example, our consciousness will move back to our driving once we realize that we've been daydreaming for a while. Indeed, our consciousness frequently moves from one purpose to another as we go about our daily activities. While we are driving the car our consciousness might move from the lane we are trying to stay in, to the reason why we are driving down the street (perhaps to get to work), to the reason we are driving to work (in order to make a living), and so on. That is, consciousness can move to a 'point of view' on our controlling that lets us become aware of *why* we are carrying out a partic- ular purpose. Consciousness can also move in the other direction, so to speak, to see *how* we are achieving our purposes. For example, while we are driving the car, our con- sciousness can move from what we are doing to keep the car in its lane (moving the steering wheel), to what we are doing to move the steering wheel (exerting forces on the wheel).

The Ghost Outside the Machine

So we know two things about consciousness simply because we ourselves are conscious beings. First, we know that consciousness is separate from purposefulness. We can carry out our purposes — we can do our controlling — consciously or unconsciously. Second, the point of view from which we are conscious of our purposes while we are carrying them out can change. Since our purposeful behavior is produced by a hierarchy of control systems consciousness can take the point of view of a lower level system and 'look up' to see why we are carrying out a particular purpose, or it can take the point of view of a higher level system and 'look down' to see how we are doing it.

We think of consciousness as being somewhat like a searchlight that scans over the different control systems in the control hierarchy looking for problems: problems such as control systems that are not controlling well; that are experiencing chronic error. If the control hierarchy is the 'machine' that produces our purposeful behavior, consciousness is like a 'ghost' that sits outside of that machine — the ghost that is the part of us that can become aware of our own controlling. We call consciousness a 'ghost' because, unlike the control hierarchy, we don't know much about how consciousness is implemented in the brain and nervous system. That is, we don't know much about the 'hardware' of consciousness though, as anyone who has experienced total anesthesia knows, consciousness is there, in the hardware, because you can remove it temporarily by drenching the hardware in an anesthetic.

The ghost of consciousness can be a very friendly ghost because it can guide the random fiddling of the reorganization process to the control systems that really need fixing, making the process much more efficient. We will see that this aspect of consciousness is what helps us solve our psychological problems. When consciousness guides reorganization to the right place, the random 'fiddlings' of the reorganization process will change the control systems that actually need to be changed. But the ghost of consciousness can also be a somewhat unfriendly ghost when it guides reorganization to control systems that are already working well. This is what is going on when we become 'self-conscious' and things that we used to be able to do perfectly well suddenly become nearly impossible. For example, this is what is going on when you go to a job interview and find your consciousness focused on what you are saying to the interviewer. Suddenly you find that your ability to form coherent sentences has disappeared. What is happening is that your consciousness has focused the reorganization process on one of the control systems in your control hierarchy that controls perfectly well — the control system that controls your perception of the sentences you are speaking. The reorganization process is making random changes to that already well functioning control system with the result that any changes that are made to this system will make it work less well.

A college professor once said that, when he was playing college basketball, before a player from the opposing team was about to take a free shot, he would ask his opponent whether he breathed in or out as he was releasing the ball. Perhaps the professor was exaggerating his influence but he said that this simple question invariably interrupted the opponent's rhythm and subsequent shooting accuracy. We can understand this result from a PCT perspective since the professor's question would have had the effect of directing the opponent's consciousness to his lower level systems controlling his breathing and ball release systems. With consciousness shining a light here, the reorganization system will commence its fiddling but fiddling down here is unnecessary and will disrupt what is otherwise good control.

The negative effect that consciousness can have on our ability to carry out our purposes skillfully — on our ability to control — was apparently noticed long ago by Zen masters. One of the goals of Zen practice is to 'become one' with what you are doing. You do this by not thinking about (i.e., not being conscious of) what you are doing. The 'one' you are 'leaving out' when you 'become one' with what you are doing is your consciousness. 'Becoming one' is, therefore, a nice way of describing how it feels to be completely in control without any awareness of how this controlling is being done. It's the feeling that an opera diva has as she floats gracefully through the high notes of an aria. It's the feeling that the tennis star has when making a perfect cross court volley. When you have learned to do something very skillfully — when you are completely in control of your song or your tennis stroke — you do it best when you do it without being conscious of how you are doing it. And the experience of 'becoming one' with something that you can do very skillfully is extremely gratifying, which is surely why it is a state recommended by the Zen masters.

The Zen emphasis on the negative effects of consciousness should not lead you to conclude that consciousness always gets in the way of controlling. Consciousness is a hindrance when it directs reorganization to control systems that are already working well. But consciousness is a help when it directs reorganization to the control systems that are not working well. So the Zen in the art of motorcycle maintenance — when the motorcycle is your own control hierarchy — is to try to keep your consciousness away from your skillful controlling and focused on the controlling that you do poorly. We will see that the skill of maintaining the 'motorcycle' of your control hierarchy is to use consciousness to direct reorganization to the places that need it, and away from the places that don't. It turns out that this is not always easy to do and is the reason why psychotherapy can be a big help in fixing psychological problems. In a later chapter we will describe a psychotherapeutic procedure called the Method of Levels (MOL) that is based on an understanding of how consciousness directs reorganization to systems in the control hierarchy that have lost control. MOL is a psychotherapy that helps people direct their consciousness to the places in their control hierarchy that need to be fixed and away from those that don't. It is a therapy that is based on an understanding of Zen and the art of controlling.

Ultimate Purposes

At the end of the last chapter we said that the goals for the control systems at the top of the control hierarchy — control systems that control for complex perceptions such as the kind of person you want to be — could not be changed by a higher level control system because there is no higher level control system there to change them. But while the goals of these top level control systems rarely change, they sometimes do change. So there must be something in us that can change them. According to PCT that 'something' is the reorganization system.

The idea that the reorganization system can change our highest level goals follows from the concept of reorganization as a process of reducing error by fiddling with components of the control systems in that hierarchy. And among the components of these control systems that the reorganization system can fiddle with, and, thus change, are the highest level goals of the control hierarchy. But recall that the goals of a control system are changed only for a higher level reason — that is, to achieve a still higher level goal. So the reorganization system must have a higher level reason for changing the highest level goals of the control hierarchy. According to PCT, the higher level reason for changing our highest level goals is to reduce the error in control systems that are controlling variables that are essential to our very survival. These are physiological variables such as body temperature, blood glucose level, and stress level. These are called *intrinsic* controlled variables because keeping these variables under control is essential for our survival. Thus, keeping intrinsic variables in their reference states is really our ultimate purpose. All the controlling we do — all the controlling done by the control hierarchy — must, in the end, result in keeping the intrinsic variables in their reference states.

The relationship between the controlling done by the hierarchy of control systems, and the state of intrinsic controlled variables is somewhat indirect, but essential. For example, your control hierarchy controls for the kind of clothes you wear and when you wear them, resulting in your 'dressing' behavior. This dressing behavior is clearly related to the state of at least one important intrinsic controlled variable — your body temperature. So your body temperature is to some extent dependent on your dressing behavior.[3] The control hierarchy is also responsible for the kind of food you eat and when you eat it. That is, the control hierarchy is responsible for your eating behavior, which is clearly related to the state of another important intrinsic controlled variable — your blood glucose level. So your blood glucose level is to some extent dependent on your eating behavior.

Indeed, all the purposeful behavior produced by the control hierarchy can have some effect on intrinsic controlled variables. This includes the behavior carried out by the highest level control systems in the control hierarchy — what you do to be the kind of person you want to be. If, for example, you want to be the kind of person who lives it up, a bon vivant, with purposes such as eating habits, that push intrinsic variables such as blood sugar level away from their reference levels, you may end up experiencing chronic *intrinsic error* — a chronic difference between the actual and reference level of an intrinsic controlled variable. This is a situation where your very survival may depend on your ability to change the goals at the top of your control hierarchy — lifestyle goals that are creating intrinsic error. Since the removal of intrinsic error is the job of the reorganization system, the aspect of you that would be responsible for changing these top level goals is the reorganization system. So the only thing that can change your highest level goals — your goals regarding the kind of person you want to be — is the reorganization system. And such change will only occur if carrying out your highest level purposes has created intrinsic error — and if the reorganization system is able to come up with a solution in time (before the intrinsic error makes survival itself impossible).

Too Much of Nothing

The reorganization system deals with intrinsic error in the same way it deals with error in the control hierarchy, using the biased random walk approach of the E. coli bacterium. This means that people who are experiencing persistent intrinsic error will appear to be behaving rather erratically as their reorganization system experiments with new ways of behaving (controlling). This is, indeed, what we see with laboratory animals that are prevented from using their usual means of obtaining food. As the period of food deprivation (and, presumably the amount of intrinsic error) increases, the animal's behavior becomes more and more erratic. In people, deprivation that increases intrinsic error will result in all kinds of changes in their behavior, which includes changes in the goals they want to achieve (the perceptions they want to control). If intrinsic error is large and persistent enough, this can include changes in one's highest level goals — goals for the kind of person one wants to be or how one wants to live one's life. If the behavior resulting from these changes decreases the intrinsic error, then the changes can become permanent. Deprivation that produces persistent intrinsic error can change a person completely. Or, as the song says:

> *Too much of nothing*
> *Can turn a man into a liar*
> *It can cause one man to sleep on nails*
> *And another man to eat fire*[4]

So the reorganization system is the part of us that is always working to reduce the difference between the way things are (our perceptions) and the way they should be (our references or goals for those perceptions). That is, it is always working to reduce error. It does this by randomly fiddling with the components of our control hierarchy in order to get us to control in a way that keeps error as small as possible. Because the reorganization process is random, the reorganization system can't know in advance which way of controlling will lead to a reduction in error. And it doesn't have to know. All the reorganization system has to know is that a particular set of 'fiddlings' results in a way of controlling (behaving) that reduces error and another doesn't. The reorganization system doesn't know whether it has come up with the best way of reducing error or the only way. And it doesn't care. All the reorganization system cares about is reducing error and whatever way it stumbles upon that works to do that is the way that will persist. In other words, the reorganization system doesn't care what it does to reduce error, it just cares that the error is reduced. This characteristic of reorganization has important implications for understanding how people are able to control other people's behavior, which we discuss in the next chapter.

Chapter 6

People Who Control People (Including Themselves)

Now that we know what controlling is and how it works, we can take a look at what is going on when controlling involves the control of other controllers. That is, we will look at what is happening when people try to control other people (including themselves). People try to control other people for the same reason that they try to control anything, such as the location of furniture in the living room or the position of their car on the road. They do it because they have reference signals in their brain that specify the 'right' way for people to behave. For example, they have references for the right foods for their child to be eating or for the right things for their spouse to be saying. So when we see that another person is not behaving the way they should be — when their behavior does not match our reference specification for how they should be behaving — there is an error signal which drives us to do things to try to correct that error. And what we do is act to try to get the person to behave the way they should (from our perspective) so as to reduce our error signal.

So controlling other people comes as naturally to us as controlling the location of our furniture or our car. In this way, being a person who wants to control other people is neither good nor bad; it is a natural consequence of one's nature as a controlling person. It would be as impossible for us to stop wanting to control other people as it is to stop wanting to control the position of your car when you are driving down the highway. But, unlike controlling furniture or cars, controlling other people can create problems for both the person doing the controlling and the person being controlled. Cars don't care that they are being controlled. Other people frequently do. Controlling a car never interferes with the nature of the car but controlling other people often interferes with the nature of the person. So it would be nice if controlling other people were really impossible. But it's not. So not only does our human nature make it impossible to stop wanting to control other people, the occasional success we have at doing this seems to support our belief that we should be doing it. In this chapter we will explain why people who control often seem to be able to get other controlling people to behave as they want — to control them. In the next chapter we will explain why problems arise when we do this.

Controlling Other People

From the point of view of a person doing the controlling, there is really no difference between controlling another control system, such as another person, and controlling something that is not a control system, such as a car. In both cases, a variable is being brought to some goal state and kept there, protected from disturbances. The variable controlled when controlling a car might be its position on the road; the variable controlled when controlling another person might be the time spent helping with the dishes. And the mechanism of control is the same in both cases as well. The person doing the controlling is acting to keep a perception of the controlled variable in the goal state that they, themselves, have selected.

The goal state selected for the position of the car is 'in the lane'; the goal state selected for time spent helping with the dishes is 'until they are finished'.

The only difference between getting a car to stay in its lane and getting a person to help with the dishes is that the car is not a control system and the person is. But surprisingly this seems to make little difference. We seem to be able to sometimes control people almost as well as we can control cars. This may seem surprising after all we have said about control systems being autonomous. But recall that control systems are only *relatively* autonomous. They do set their own goals for the perceptions they want to control, but once a goal is set, that pretty much determines what actions the control system must take to achieve it. And there lies the tool that a person can use to control another person. If you can determine what goal a person is trying to achieve, then you can control the person's behavior by arranging things so that they can achieve their goal only by doing what you want them to do. That is, you can get a person to do what you want by making sure that they only get what they want by doing what you want. This is the basis of what is probably the most common approach to controlling behavior — giving and withholding rewards or, as they are called in the behavior control literature, *reinforcements*. The problem with dealing with people using this 'carrots and sticks' approach to behavior control will be discussed in Chapter 10.

Do What I Want to Get What You Want

From a PCT perspective, reinforcement is the reference or goal state of a perceptual variable or, more simply, it is what a control system, like a person, wants, that it doesn't yet have. Something is reinforcing only if a person wants it and doesn't have it (or doesn't have enough of it). This is why something can be a reinforcement to one person and not another. It is also why something can be a reinforcement to a person at one time but not at another. Food, for example, is reinforcement to a person who is hungry but not to one who is full. This is why the first step in using reinforcements to control someone is to make sure that what you plan to use as a reinforcement is something that the person wants and doesn't have enough of.

Once you know what a person wants (and doesn't have) the next step is to ensure that the only way for them to get it is by doing what you want them to do. This is the crucial step in controlling behavior using reinforcements. And it can be the most difficult step depending on who you are planning to control and what it is you are planning to use as reinforcement. The difficulty turns on your ability to prevent the controlee from getting the reinforcement in some way other than how you want them to get it. For example, if you want to use treats as reinforcements for doing homework then you have to arrange things so that there is no other way for the controlee to get the treats other than by doing homework. It's probably easier to do this if the controlee is a young child (who can't get to the store to buy the treats himself) than a teenager (who can probably find other ways to get the treats). If you want to use loving words as reinforcements for washing the dishes then you have to arrange things so that there is no way for the controlee to get those words other than by doing the dishes. In this case the difficulty probably depends more on your ability to give and withhold the loving words appropriately than on the age of the controlee.

Controlled By Contingency

Once you have found a reinforcement and arranged things so that the controlee can get it only by doing what you want, you are ready to start controlling. The process involves making the reinforcement *contingent* on the occurrence of the behavior you want to see performed. This means that you can give the reinforcement only after the controlee has done what you want them to do. But the controlee may never do exactly what you want so you could be waiting forever to give the reinforcement. Even if you tell the controlee what you want them to do they may not do exactly what you want or simply ignore you. For example, if you tell a child to go to their room and do homework for an hour they may go to their room and not do homework or not go to their room at all. The solution to this problem is to use a procedure that Skinner called *shaping*, which involves reinforcing successive approximations to the behavior you want to see.

Skinner viewed the process of shaping behavior as being similar to the process of shaping a sculpture. In both cases you gradually get to the desired 'shape' by taking small steps in the right direction. With the sculpture, the small steps are taken by removing only those parts of a block of marble that are not part of the final sculpture. With behavior, the small steps are taken by keeping only those parts of what a person is doing that are part of the final behavior. And shaping behavior takes nearly as much skill as shaping a sculpture. Skinner himself was quite skillful at shaping behavior. He was able to get pigeons to play ping pong with each other and, as we noted earlier, he was able to get Erich Fromm to chop the air with his hand during a talk. In both cases Skinner used shaping to get organisms (pigeons and a person) to behave in ways that are quite different from the ways they ordinarily behave.

The art of shaping is being able to pick from what the controlee is doing only those behaviors that are closer and closer approximations to the final behavior you want to see. At the start of the process you have to pick a behavior that looks like part of the final behavior. For example, in order to get a left-hand chopping motion from Fromm, Skinner probably started by looking for any kind of movement of Fromm's left hand. As soon as he saw such a movement Skinner would give Fromm a reinforcement by paying attention to him briefly. The reinforcement should result in a repetition of the movement — it 'strengthens' the behavior. Once this first approximation to the final behavior is strengthened sufficiently — it has been repeated enough times — reinforcement is withheld until an even closer approximation to the final behavior occurs. So, once Fromm's slight left hand movement has occurred often enough, Skinner would stop paying attention to Fromm — withholding reinforcement — until Fromm did something that was an even closer approximation to the desired 'chopping' behavior. When this closer approximation occurs, it is reinforced until it is sufficiently strengthened, at which point reinforcement is again withheld until a still closer approximation to the desired final behavior is seen. This process of giving and withholding reinforcement after successively closer approximations continues until the final desired behavior is seen, at which point the shaping has been successful.

The Man Behind the Curtain

One of Skinner's most interesting discoveries was a phenomenon that he called 'superstitious behavior'. It is seen when an animal is given reinforcements at regular intervals, regardless of what it is doing before each reinforcement arrives. The situation is almost the opposite of what is done when shaping behavior. Rather than making reinforcement contingent on closer and closer approximations to some particular behavior, as in shaping, reinforcement in the 'superstitious behavior' situation is contingent on whatever the animal happens to be doing just before each reinforcement is delivered. The result of this process is that some behavior — the one that, by chance, happens to be most often followed by a reinforcement — ends up becoming the one that is 'shaped' into a final form. The behaviors that are shaped by this process can be quite odd. For example, in a 'superstitious behavior' study using pigeons, Skinner found that one bird always made two or three counter-clockwise turns before the reinforcement arrived; another repeatedly thrust its head into an upper corner of the cage prior to reinforcement. These behaviors look a lot like the superstitious routines that some baseball or tennis players go through before starting play. Indeed, the superstitious behavior of these players is probably the result of the same kind of rein-forcement contingencies that produced this behavior in pigeons; it's the behavior that happened to be followed most often by a reinforcement, such as a hit or an ace.

The phenomenon of 'superstitious behavior' seems to show that behavior can be shaped without anyone there to do the shaping. That is, behavior seems to be controlled by rein-forcements alone, even if these reinforcements are delivered blindly by a machine, with no one there to make them con-tingent on the occurrence of some particular behavior. If this were actually the case it would mean that a person who is shaping behavior is doing nothing different than what the reinforcements would be doing on their own if the person were not there to deliver them. This is certainly the way Skinner saw things. When Skinner was shaping Fromm's behavior, for example, he assumed that he was doing exactly what the reinforcements would have been doing if he were not delivering them himself. The only difference, from Skinner's perspective, was that he wanted to pick the behaviors to be shaped rather than leave it up to the random occurrence of the reinforcements. But this is the difference that makes all the difference. The difference between the shaping done by Skinner and that done by the reinforcements is that while

Skinner can pick the behavior he wants to see performed, the reinforcements can't.

Skinner is able to control behavior because he is a control system; the reinforcements are not. Because he is a control system Skinner is able to set goals for the behavior he wants to perceive and can act to get his perception of behavior to the goal state; the reinforcements can't. Skinner is actually using the reinforcements as the means of getting behavior to a goal state — the reference state that Skinner himself has defined by setting a reference for the perception of that behavior. And Skinner is using the reinforcements in exactly the way a control system uses its outputs to coax a controlled variable to the reference or goal state. This can be seen in the way Skinner shaped Fromm's 'chopping' behavior. The controlled variable is the movement of Fromm's left hand. Skinner's goal for this variable was 'chopping the air'. Skinner achieved this goal by varying his 'outputs' by delivering reinforcements when Fromm's movements were approaching the 'chopping' goal and withholding them when they were not.

In saying that 'reinforcements control behavior' Skinner was saying something like what the Wizard of Oz said when he was discovered pulling the levers that actually created all the magic in the land of Oz: 'Pay no attention to the man behind the curtain'. Skinner is the man behind the curtain using reinforcements to control behavior. The reinforcements themselves don't control behavior because they don't want people (or other animals) to behave in any particular way. Only a living control system — a controlling person — can control behavior, because only a living control system can want people to behave in a particular way. Skinner thought he had discovered that reinforcements control behavior when he had actually discovered that he himself was the one doing the controlling. Skinner had discovered his own nature as a purposeful, controlling person but ignored it. He was committed to the idea that when he was controlling behavior he wasn't doing anything that couldn't also be done by reinforcements alone.

Why It Works

Even though Skinner was wrong about reinforcements being what controls behavior, he was right about the fact that behavior — that of both animals (like the ping pong playing pigeons) and people (like the psychologist Erich Fromm) — can be controlled. And Skinner described how it can be done by reinforcing successive approximations to the target behavior. But now the question is 'why does this work'? Why are we able to control someone who is just as much 'in control' as we are? When we control another person we seem to be in the paradoxical situation of the character of Henry Higgins, denying our own ability to be in control by treating a person just like us as though they are not in control themselves. But it turns out that we are able to control other people *because* they are able to be in control, just like we are. That is, we can control other people because they, like us, are controlling people.

The ability to control another person takes advantage of the fact that a control system only cares about what it gets, not how it gets it. What a control system gets is a perception of the state of a controlled variable, such as a perception of hunger. What it cares about is keeping that perception at a reference or goal level. In the case of hunger, this means that the control system only cares about keeping the perception of hunger at zero: not hungry. What the control system doesn't care about is what it has to do to get a perception to the reference level. In the case of hunger, this means that the control system doesn't care what it has to do to keep hunger at the reference of zero — whether it is has to feed itself with a knife and fork, chopsticks, or by pressing a bar. Similarly, a teacher in a class-room doesn't necessarily care how they keep the noise level at a volume they are satisfied with. They might frown or smile or clear their throat or move around the room or give warnings or offer incentives or a myriad of other things to keep the sounds in the room as they like them to be.

Control systems control what they perceive, not what they do. Actually, we already saw that this is the case when we discussed the relative autonomy of a control system. We saw that once a control system has 'freely' (autonomously) selected a reference level for a particular perception it is no longer free to select what it will do to keep that perception at the reference level. What a control system has to do to keep a perception at the reference level is determined by the nature of the world in which the system does its controlling. In order keep a perception of hunger at the reference level, the control system has to eat, and if it lives in a world where the only way to eat is with a knife and fork, then it will act to control hunger by eating with a knife and fork; if it lives in a world where the only way to eat is with chopsticks then it will act to control hunger by eating with chopsticks; and if it lives in a world where the only way to eat is by pressing a bar in a Skinner box then it will act to control hunger by pressing a bar.

So you can control the behavior of a control system by arranging the world so that the only way it can control a perception is by doing what you want to see it doing. This is how Skinner controlled the behavior of rats in a Skinner box and the behavior of Erich Fromm at a conference. The first step was to identify a controlled variable. For the rats it was hunger; for Fromm it was being attended to by Skinner. The next step was to make sure that this variable was not currently at its reference level. For the rats, this was done by starving them (bringing them to 80% of their normal body weight);

for Fromm, this was done by ignoring him until he chopped the air with his hand. The next step was to set up the world so that the only way for the controlee to control the controlled variable was to do what Skinner wanted to see done. For the rats, this was done by putting them in a cage (the Skinner box) where the only way to control hunger was by pressing a bar; for Fromm, this was done by making it so that the only way to control for Skinner paying attention was to chop the air with his left hand.

This PCT-based analysis of how you can control the behavior of a control system leads to the somewhat counter-intuitive conclusion that you have to give a control system control of a perception in order to get control of your perception of its behavior. That might sound a bit convoluted so let's say it another way: In order to control the behavior of another controller, you have to let the controller control. Or as the great Zen teacher Shunryu Suzuki said: 'To give your sheep or cow a large, spacious meadow is the way to control him'[1]. Skinner had to give the rat control of its perception of hunger, by providing the 'spacious meadow' of the Skinner box, in order to be able to control the rat's bar pressing behavior. He had to give Fromm control of his perception of Skinner's attention by providing the 'spacious meadow' of Fromm's gesticulating, in order to be able to control Fromm's chopping-the-air behavior.

When we look at it this way, control of behavior doesn't seem like such a bad thing; we may be taking something from you by controlling a perception of your behavior but we are giving something in return by giving you control of a perception you want (or need) to control. But this congenial view of behavior control fails to take into account the fact that people contain multitudes of control systems. So even though we are controlling your behavior by giving you the ability to control a perception you want (or need) to control, other control systems in you may be controlling for perceiving that you are not being controlled. These systems can see that we are controlling you — that you are being 'played' — and this creates an error that drives actions that resist our controlling. The result is a conflict between the controller (or controllers) and the would-be controlee. This creates problems for both the controller and controlee and it is the main reason why controlling the behavior of other control systems — other people — is usually a bad idea.

Control by Deception

There is another approach to controlling behavior that should be mentioned because it is a very popular approach to controlling groups of people. This form of control takes advantage of the 'disturbance resisting' aspect of the behavior of controlling people. It involves lying about the existence of a disturbance to a controlled variable — a disturbance that doesn't exist. This approach to controlling behavior is apparently learned at a very young age. When my (RSM) daughter was three years old she was able to get a swing away from her six year old brother by telling him 'Mommy is calling you'. My daughter apparently knew that Mommy's call would be a disturbance to a perception controlled by her brother — going to Mommy when he called — and that this disturbance would have to be corrected by the brother leaving the swing to go find Mommy. And sure enough, her brother went to find Mommy, freeing up the swing for her. Of course, Mommy wasn't really calling. A similar situation happens on a large scale in the last few months of every year when many parents (at least in the Western world) tell their children that Santa Claus won't be calling unless they are 'good'.

This method of control is effective when you can correctly guess at what perception a person is controlling and what the person would have to do to correct for a disturbance to that perception. Political propagandists are particularly good at this, being able to control the behavior of large groups of people by correctly guessing what perceptions most people in the group are controlling for and what they would do to correct for a disturbance to that perception. While this method of control can be very effective, it can usually be used only once. My daughter's approach to getting the swing from her brother worked that once but as soon as her brother found out that Mommy was not calling him, it could no longer be used in the future. The Santa Claus method of control can only be used while children believe in Santa Claus (or at least give the impression that they believe). The same is true of political propaganda, although the propagandists are very good at determining other perceptions that people control and creating new lies about non-existent disturbances to those perceptions. So controlling people's behavior using deception will surely be around for a long time to come. The only way to stop it is to control the behavior of the propagandists, which creates its own problems — problems that result from living in the paradox of controlling people.

I Control, Therefore I Am Controllable

When we control behavior using reinforcements or deception we are taking advantage of the fact that a person we are controlling is a control system. We can control a person using reinforcements because the person is trying to control those reinforcements. We control a person using deception because the person is trying to control something that we are falsely claiming is out of control. So we are able to control people *because* those people are trying to be in control. And since the people who are busy controlling other people are themselves controlling people, they are just as controllable as the people they control. This is demonstrated by a phenomenon called *counter-control* that was observed by one of the authors (TAC) in the context of observing behavior in a classroom. The teacher in a classroom wants, among other things, to maintain a calm learning environment, which means keeping the students 'under control'. When a student acts up in class the teacher has to take steps to counter the disturbance. If the teacher is what is known as a *high gain* controller these steps might involve screaming and wild gesturing aimed at getting the student to quiet down. But these types of effort to control obstreperous students made the teacher a target of the students, who knew they could get the teacher to scream and gesture wildly by simply acting up in class. The students took advantage of the teacher's controlling to control the teacher.

So a PCT understanding of people as controllers shows that we can be controlled *because* we control. This controllability is limited, though, since we can only be made to do what we would ordinarily do to counter disturbances to the perceptions we are controlling. We can be made to yell and gesture wildly by an obstreperous student only if that is the means we use to control student behavior. We can't be made to yell and gesture wildly if that is not the way we deal with misbehavior. Our controllability is also limited by the fact that we can often see that we are being controlled and we can take steps to avoid it. For example, the high gain teacher who notices that he or she is being controlled (made a fool of) by the obstreperous student can stop being controlled by simply giving up her efforts to control the obstreperous student and have others handle it.

The ultimate way to become uncontrollable is to stop controlling. This would require us to stop wanting anything at all, including air, food, and shelter. In other words, it would require us to stop living, which is a fairly extreme approach to avoid being controlled. So in order to continue as a living, controlling person it looks like we will have to accept the fact that we not only have to deal with our natural inclination to control other people but also with the fact that this same inclination makes us controllable.

A PCT understanding of the nature of control shows that being in control and being controlled are not incompatible at all. Indeed, PCT shows that people are most controllable when they are in control. This is just the way control works. When you are controlling some perception someone else can control you by creating disturbances that require you to act to protect that perception from those disturbances. It's the actions you use to protect the controlled perception from the disturbance that can be controlled. That's what is going on with the teacher and the obstreperous student. The teacher's actions can be controlled by creating a disturbance to a perception that the teacher is protecting from disturbance by taking those actions.

Behave, Damn It!

When it is not possible to get someone to do what you want by disturbing a controlled perception, very high gain controlling people will resort to the ultimate (and most brutal) way of controlling other people — the use of physical force. There is no subtlety involved in this kind of control. It does not take advantage of any aspects of a person as a controller. It simply involves treating the person as a physical object and using overwhelming force to make the controlee act as desired. Since the controlee is likely to push pack as hard as possible against the person trying to control them, this approach to controlling behavior is the most violent and unattractive. But it is not always seen as wrong. For example, control by force is used when we prevent a three year old from chasing a ball into the street. Since an adult can easily overpower the child, this kind of control can be quite successful, which is a good thing since the adult knows more than the child about the possible consequences of running into the street.

Control by force becomes the most violent and is typically viewed as most wrong when the controller and controlee are more equal in size and cognitive ability than the adult and child. But this is the approach to control that is too often taken when people persist in their goal of getting someone to do what they want. When bribery (contingencies of reinforcement) and deception (falsely disturbing a controlled variable) fail, control by force is the last resort if the controller is unwilling (or unable) to give up the goal of having the controlee behave as desired.

Self-Control

We will discuss in more detail the problems associated with controlling other people in the next chapter. But for now there is one more important point to make about control systems controlling other control systems. Up to now we have been assuming that the control system doing the controlling (the controller) and the control system being controlled (the controlee) are in two separate organisms (two different people or a person and another animal). However very often the controller and controlee control systems are in the same person. When this is the case it is called *self-control*, which is a kind of misnomer because it's not a 'self' that is being controlled but another control system within one's self.

An example of self-control is dieting. Here we have two different control systems, one of which is controlling for reducing our eating (call it the diet control system) and the other controlling for eating as usual (the hunger control system). Both control systems are in the same person — you, the one on a diet. The diet control system is the controller in this situation because it wants to control (that is, stop or at least reduce) the eating behavior of the hunger control system. It can do this in the same way that it would control the behavior of another person; it can use contingencies of reinforcement. So your diet control system might tell your eating control system that it will reward it with something it likes — a cookie, perhaps — if it doesn't eat anything all day. That is, you, as the diet control system, can bargain with yourself, as the hunger control system, to try to get the hunger control system to behave the way you want.

So 'bargaining with oneself' is one approach to 'self-control' — to controlling one's own behavior. It is essentially equivalent to the *control by reinforcement contingency* approach used to control the behavior of other people. But the more common approach to self-control is to use what is basically brute force where the controller control system in you virtually grabs the controlee system by the throat and forces it to behave as desired. In the dieting situation the diet control system tries to control the hunger control system by forcing it to not eat. This is self-control by 'willpower'. What is actually happening, though, has more to do with controlling than willing. In order to see what is going on when we exert self-control through 'willpower' we have to understand the concept of control system *gain*.

The Importance of Gain

The *gain* of a control system refers to how much output the system produces per unit error. That is, gain is measured in terms of how much 'oomph' a control system puts out per unit increase in the discrepancy between the state of the controlled variable and the reference for the state of that variable. A high gain control system is one that produces a lot of oomph per unit error; a low gain control system produces very little oomph per unit error. For example, a high gain thermostat has a very powerful furnace (and air conditioner) so that even a small deviation of room temperature from the reference ('set point') temperature results in a lot of heating (if the room temperature goes below the set point) or cooling (if the room temperature goes above the set point). You might think that such a strong output would cause an overshoot with a small amount of error. For example, the room temperature dips slightly below the set point and results in a strong reaction — the heater comes on full blast — which pushes the controlled variable too far in the opposite direction — the heater output drives the room temperature way over the set point. But this doesn't happen because the control system's output occurs in a closed negative feedback loop. So the high gain output quickly pushes the error back to zero — bringing the controlled variable back to the reference (set point) level — so that the output is stopped and there is no overshoot. The result is that a control system with high gain controls better than one with low gain. The control exerted by a high gain control system is 'tighter' than that of a low gain system in the sense that a high gain system keeps the controlled variable more tightly aligned with the reference specification for that variable than does a low gain system.

In a person who contains multitudes of control systems, the perceptions controlled by high gain control systems can be considered more important to the person than those con-trolled by low gain ones. If the perception of dieting is controlled with higher gain than the perception of hunger, then control of dieting can be considered more important to the person than control of hunger. This is relevant to self-control because a high gain control system can overpower a low gain one. If dieting is more important than not being hungry then the diet control system can overpower the hunger control system and effectively control its behavior. The person will seem to have exhibited self-control through willpower. But it is actually a stronger, higher gain control system overpowering a weaker, lower gain one.

It's important to understand that this is what is going on with a brute force approach to self-control because it explains why willpower so often fails. It fails because even though the controlee control system is low gain, it has some gain, which is better than no gain at all. The oomph of the output produced by a control system is proportional to gain *times* error. This means that even a control system with low gain will produce a lot of oomph when the error in the system gets big. And the error in the controlee control system will get big as the controller continues to try to keep it from doing what it needs to do to control its own perception. Eventually, the error in the controlee becomes so big that it ends up doing what it wants — acting to get its perception under control — and the controller loses control. In the dieting situation, the high gain diet control system may be strong enough to prevent the hunger control system from eating. But while it is doing this the error in the low gain hunger control system is getting larger and larger until finally the product of gain times error is enough to drive its output. Willpower suddenly seems to fail as the hunger control system starts shoving food in like there is no tomorrow. But it's not willpower that has failed — the power (gain) of the diet control system is still just as high as it was. It is the weaker controlee system that has succeeded, at least for the time being, at getting its own perception under control thanks to the increased error created by the 'willpower' of the stronger, diet control system.

The difference in gain between control systems within the same person, like that between the diet and hunger control systems, can explain some of the different manifestations of psychological distress. When the internal dispute between control systems involves systems with very different gains there will be periods of successful 'willpower' followed by episodes of 'relapse' or 'rebound'. When both control systems have high gain, however, there will be sustained experiences of debilitating indecision and instability. Both of these problems are commonly observed in people who are trying to improve themselves using 'self-control'.

So now we have described how control systems can control each other's behavior, whether those systems are in different people or in the same person. The goal here was simply to show that PCT can explain what we see people doing all the time. We see people controlling other people — sometimes successfully and sometimes not — and controlling themselves using self-control. But the fact that people can control other people (and themselves) doesn't mean that they should be doing it. We have hinted at the problems that could result when we try to control others and ourselves. In the next chapter we will give a more detailed explanation of what those problems are.

Chapter 7

Conflict: People at Cross Purposes

The Nature of Conflict

A conflict exists when two or more control systems try to bring the same perceptual variable to different goal or reference states. A simple example of a conflict is what happens when two people push on opposite sides of a swinging door. One person is entering the room and is controlling for perceiving the door opening into the room; the other person is leaving the room and is controlling for perceiving the door opening out of the room. Since the door can't be open into and out of the room at the same time, the two people cannot control their perceptions of the position of the door simultaneously. Indeed, what happens in a conflict is that a perceptual variable, like the position of the swinging door, ends up stuck between the goal states sought by the different control systems. The swinging door remains closed because the person's efforts to open it out are being resisted by the person who wants to open it in, and vice versa. As with the dieting example in the previous chapter, if one of the door pushers was much stronger (higher gain) than the other, the strong door-opener may be able to force the door open but it will still be a fairly unsatisfactory controlling. If the door-openers are equally matched in strength, the door will stay shut for as long as the pushers keep pushing. So when control systems are in conflict, neither system is able to get what it wants. The control systems that are in conflict have lost control of the perception they are trying to control; and they have lost control because they are trying to be in control — of the same perception. Conflict is, thus, that paradoxical situation where one's efforts to be in control result in the loss of control.

Conflict is something that only afflicts purposeful (control) systems. If the people involved in the door conflict were not purposeful systems but just weights purposelessly pushing the door from opposite directions there would be no conflict. Since the weights have no goals, they don't care what happens to the door — whether it is pushed into or out of the room. If one weight were heavier and, thus, pushed harder on the door than the other, then the door would open away from the heavier weight. But when there are purposeful systems involved, the pushes of one system will be resisted by the pushing back of the other. This is because the pushes of each system are a disturbance to the perception controlled by the other. The result is that both systems will end up pushing hard in opposite directions and the door stays put. If the conflict persists, the two people will remain pushing on the door in opposite directions. Neither will ever achieve their goal. Their continued efforts to control the position of the door will keep them from being able to control the position of the door.

When people are in conflict, they are truly at cross purposes. The people on each side of the swinging door are at cross purposes in the sense that their purposes work against each other and prevent them from achieving those purposes. Conflict is always a possibility when many control systems are operating in the same environment at the same time, as is the case in a society where many people — or many control systems within the same person — are all doing their controlling in pretty much the same place at the same time. For example, because several people cannot occupy the same position on the road at the same time there will be conflict when several people want to use the same freeway entrance at the same time. Also, because you can't both eat and not eat at the same time, there will be conflict when you want to both eat your cake (because you are hungry) and not eat it too (because you are on a diet).

Ingredients of Conflict

One kind of conflict — like the one between drivers trying to get on the same freeway entrance at the same time — is called an *interpersonal* conflict because it is a conflict between control systems that are inside different people. The other kind of conflict — like the one between the systems trying to ignore and satisfy hunger at the same time — is called an *intrapersonal* conflict because it is a conflict between control systems within the same person. But whether the conflict is interpersonal or intrapersonal, the ultimate cause of the conflict is the same. It results when two or more control systems share the same environment. In particular, conflict results when two or more control systems are trying to get the same aspect of the environment into different, incompatible goal states at the same time — a physical impossibility.

So, one of the main ingredients of conflict is a *shared environment*. Ironically, another important ingredient of conflict is that the control systems involved need to be very good controllers. Control systems that control very well and keep errors very small are much more likely to become embroiled in conflicts than those that control poorly. Since the higher the gain of a control system the better the control system controls, conflict between high gain control systems is likely to be more debilitating and longer lasting than conflict between low gain control systems or between a high gain and a low gain control system.

The ingredients of a good, strong conflict, therefore, are a shared environment, high gain, and the impossible insistence that one aspect of that environment be in different, incompatible states simultaneously. Given these three requirements and the number of expert (high gain) controllers there are on the planet (and inside of oneself) it is no surprise that conflict happens as frequently as it does.

Environments of Conflict

Conflict is likely whenever control systems share an environment, but some environments lend themselves more readily to conflict than others. The environments that are most conducive to conflict are places where control of behavior is necessary. In schools, for example, it is not uncommon for teachers to spend a large part of the day specifying how students should sit, how noisy they should be, the work they should do, and so on. Sometimes choices are offered but these can actually increase the likelihood of conflict rather than decrease it. With a choice such as 'You can finish your math now or come back at lunch time and finish it' it is perhaps easy to see how this can lead to conflict. However, even a choice such as 'We need to do spelling and sums this morning — which one would you like to do first?' can be problematic. Perhaps neither option appeals to one or more students.

Workplaces where some people manage and supervise and other people are managed and supervised are also environments that are ideal breeding grounds for conflicts. In this situation both the manager and the managed share the same environment and both of them will have goals about the same variables for much of the time. On some occasions these goals might be different. Perhaps the manager thinks that customers should receive reminder text messages for their next appointment but the managed thinks that uninvited reminders are intrusive and unnecessary. In this situation, then, a conflict is likely.

When people can move in and out of environments there is a lot less likelihood of conflict than in environments where people are required, mandated, or need to be. Jails are environments like this and so are schools to a lesser extent. (We're not wanting to imply that schools are like jails but just pointing out that young people between certain ages are required by law to be at school.) In a similar way, some adult people feel trapped in jobs that they don't think they can leave because of their financial commitments to their families.

Sporting environments provide great examples of intense conflicts that only last within that environment. While sporting contests are often called 'competitions' it's not too hard to see that they meet the criteria for conflict. A sporting event is a situation where one athlete or team of athletes want the 'result' in one state while another athlete or team of athletes want the 'result' in a simultaneously incompatible state. The fact that there can only be one winner is what makes sporting events and contests so exciting. There are probably no other situations where conflicts have the prescribed beginning and ending that they do in a sporting event. Most sporting events continue until there is an eventual winner. In other conflicts, however, there is often no clear winner, just a simmering brew of mistrust and bad feelings.

Sometimes, environments appear to stay the same but people's goals within those environments change and conflict is created this way. Newlyweds can start off with similar goals — or at least thinking they have similar goals — but after a few years they might discover that different things are important to them. One member of the couple starts to realize that they have the ability to build a stellar career and receive the acknowledgement and reinforcements that they never received as a child. At the same time the other person making up the couple starts to become more and more committed to building a strong sense of family characterized by evening family meals, family holidays and drives in the country, and regular visits to aunts, uncles, and cousins. The incompatibility of 'career' and 'family' goals might not be immediately obvious but, over time, the tensions are likely to grow. The career oriented partner will need to spend more time at the office, perhaps have trips away, and attend company dinners and other functions. At times it might even be advantageous to have the other partner attend some of these functions. For the other partner, however, these career opportunities might detract from the building of strong family relationships. As more time is spent on career activities, there'll be less time for family holidays, evening meals, and so on. In fact it's likely that as the children in the family grow older it will become more important for the family oriented partner to be experiencing increasing numbers of family events but this is just the time when the career oriented partner will be wanting to be more heavily invested in career promoting activities.

Arbitrary Versus Respectful Control

Because some control of behavior is required in any environment where many different control systems interact, conflict can be expected to occur in such environments. For example, the drivers who share the environment of our street system control each other via traffic rules that are enforced by police and conflicts between drivers are not unheard of. So you may not think of yourself as a person who spends much time controlling other people but unless you are a hermit living far from other people, perhaps on a tropical island somewhere, you actually spend a large part of your day controlling other people. And other people spend a large part of their day controlling you. But it's hard to tell that this kind of controlling is going on because it is usually done in a very nonchalant, friendly kind of way without any conflict. We expect the behavior of people who are controlling other people to be loud and violent, and sometimes it is. The parent who threatens or cajoles in an attempt to get their child to do homework or to stop taking sweets from the supermarket shelf is clearly trying to control the child's behavior. The dictator who threatens dissidents by placing troops in the streets is obviously trying to control the dissidents' behavior. But most of the time, when we are controlling other people (or being controlled by them), our behavior does not look very 'controlling'.

The difference between the violent, intensely conflictive controlling of the dictator and the (usually) more gentle, non-conflictive controlling done by people driving in traffic is the difference between *arbitrary* and *respectful control* of other control systems. Arbitrary control of behavior does not take into account (or actively ignores) the fact that the person whose behavior you are controlling has their own goals regarding how they want the world to be. Respectful control is just the opposite. You control with awareness that you are dealing with a person who has their own goals about the way the world should be — a purposeful person. A person who controls arbitrarily cares only about seeing a person produce the behavior they want to see. A parent who is arbitrarily controlling a child, trying to get the child to do homework, doesn't care whether the child has other goals that might be interfered with by their doing homework. A person who controls respectfully does care about the fact that the person whose behavior they want to control has other goals. The parent who respectfully controls for the child doing homework still wants to see the child do homework but is willing to make compromises that respect the fact that there are other things the child wants as well.

Respectful control is the basis of many everyday social interactions that actually involve the control of behavior. The 'respectfulness' of the controlling is achieved, at least tacitly, through social consensus. This consensus makes the control of behavior that is going on so gentle that it doesn't seem like it is even happening because there is little or no conflict. For example, a common social interaction that involves control of behavior is that between a shopper and a cashier. Suppose you are the shopper and you purchase $35.00 worth of groceries and hand the cashier $40. The cashier then hands you back $5, you say 'thanks' and leave. It doesn't seem like much controlling was going on there but, in fact, there was. We can see this using the Test for the Controlled Variable or 'Test' that we discussed in Chapter 3. We start by noting that one possible controlled variable is the amount of change you get from the cashier. You might be controlling the cashier's change-giving behavior with the goal of keeping that behavior at 'giving the correct change'. You can do The Test as a thought experiment by imagining what you would do if the cashier gave you $1 rather than $5 in change. This would be a disturbance to the 'correct change' variable and you would surely act to correct things by letting the cashier know that you should be getting $5.

The Test can be used to show that the cashier is controlling your behavior as well. The aspect of your behavior being controlled is likely to be the amount paid for the groceries. The goal state for this variable is that you pay at least what the groceries cost. You can easily test this guess by handing the cashier $10 for the $35 groceries. The cashier will act to correct for this disturbance by asking you for $25. If you don't come up with the money you won't be allowed to take the groceries. Again, the cashier's controlling is not apparent until there is a disturbance to the controlled variable.

In the interaction between a cashier and customer, disturbances such as getting the wrong change and paying less than the required amount occur rarely so it seems like there is no control going on. But when these disturbances do occur, control will become obvious from the strong corrective actions that are taken; the short-changed customer will yell and scream, if necessary, to get the correct change, and the stiffed cashier will call the police, if necessary, to get paid for the groceries. There are many human interactions, however, where control is involved but disturbances do not necessarily result in any corrective action. One way to tell that control is involved in such interactions is to be a participant in them. For example, you have probably found yourself controlling for getting a polite nod when you pass someone on the street. You do this by making eye contact and nodding yourself. Usually the person nods back but, if not, this would be a disturbance — you are not getting the perception you want. But this rarely leads to corrective action. You don't go back and tell the person they should have nodded back. So someone watching the interaction would not be able to tell that you were actually controlling for getting the passerby to acknowledge your nod. But you yourself can tell because you would experience the error — the deviation between what you want to perceive (the person nodding back) and what you actually perceive (the person ignoring you).

Lowering the Gain

One way to keep the control of behavior in social interactions from blossoming into intense conflict is by lowering the gain when you are the system doing the controlling. It is not clear what determines the gain of human control systems — it's something inside the humans themselves — but it is clear that some controlling is much higher gain than others. This is especially clear in the examples of social control described above. The controlling done by the customer and the cashier is very high gain; even a small disturbance will result in strong corrective action. If the cashier returns $4.75 instead of $5 in change the customer is very likely to protest until the cashier returns the $0.25. If the customer pays $34 rather than the required $35 he is likely to be stopped by the cashier. The controlling you do to get a polite response from a passerby, on the other hand, is quite low gain. When there is a small or even large disturbance there is unlikely to be any corrective response. If the passerby doesn't respond politely it's just not that important to you.

It is easy to think of many other examples of social control, some high gain and some low. For example, consider what is going on when your partner asks you to do the dishes. You can use The Test to see that she is controlling with pretty high gain for seeing you do the dishes. Imagine what is likely to happen if you say 'no'. (It is probably better to do this as a thought experiment only!)

Or consider what is going on when you ask the person across the table to pass the salt. Because the person is engrossed in conversation he ignores your request. So you ask someone else or get up and get it yourself. In this case you are trying to control the person's salt passing behavior, but with fairly low gain. Indeed, this kind of social control is going on all the time in human interactions. And things generally seem to go pretty smoothly. People don't seem to be exerting any effort to be in control and they don't seem to be putting up much resistance to being controlled, which is surprising because this is not what we expect.

We don't like to be controlled and we imagine that we would resist efforts to control us. Yet we *are* being controlled — as we are when we pay for what we buy — all the time and we make no complaint at all. We also think of people who control other people (or try to) as exerting this control through threats, raised voices, and other kinds of violence. Yet we find that we are able to control people — as we do when we control the cashier —with grace and calm. This is true when control is exerted non-arbitrarily as is the case in agreed to social interactions such as the customer and cashier example, or when it is exerted with the appropriate level of gain, as in the case of asking someone to pass the salt. So we can reduce the conflicts that are possible whenever we are dealing with other controlling people by simply remembering to respect other people — to realize that they have their own goals about the way things should be — and to lower the gain when we find that we are starting to get push back from the people we are trying to control.

Control Yourself

Hostilities between people are unpleasant and disturbing but hostilities within one's head are even more debilitating. Yet internal disputes and skirmishes are very common. In fact, many conflicts that seem to be between people can actually be traced to a conflict *within* at least one of the heads of the two conflicted people. The conflict you have with your boss may actually be a conflict you are having with yourself between wanting to tell your boss exactly what you think of her pre-historic management techniques and wanting to keep your job. The battle you are having with your partner because he has let himself go and is now boring and consumed with work might really be an internal struggle between wanting to maintain the security, safety, and warmth of your marriage and wanting to take up your colleague's offer of an exciting, passionate, and romantic liaison. The cool and off-hand manner in which you are treating your loud and obnoxious dinner guest could be the best you can manage at being caught between wanting to share your views of his opinionated grandstanding and not wanting to make the evening any worse for the other guests.

Conflicts between two people certainly exist but uncomplicated strife between people actually ends fairly quickly. When two villains are in a no-holes-barred contest, things escalate quite quickly and pretty awfully and then, as suddenly as it happened, it's over, with one villain the victor. What keeps interpersonal conflict simmering over extended periods of time is usually some internal indecision or uncertainty on the part of one of the combatants. This even applies to international disputes. If one country was sufficiently irritated by another country that the irritated country wanted to obliterate its annoying terrestrial associate, they'd just send sufficient military strength to create a big hole where the bothersome country used to be and that would be that. The longevity of international warfare occurs because, at the same time that one country wants to make the other country toe the global line, they also want to observe international protocols, or preserve life, or not put themselves into impossible debt, or not create clashes with other countries, or not disrupt their trade relationships, and so on.

Internal conflict is common, pervasive, and distressing. Concern for personal maladies of a psychological nature is big business. If you take a look around your local bookstore, or on the internet you will get some sense of the proliferation of books and other resources designed to help people help themselves. You may have even bought this book in your quest to live a happier and more harmonious life.

In some ways, we could be described as living in the 'age of the self'. The 'self' has assumed an almost obsessional status in our current society. Well, in Western society anyway. There is no end of books talking about self-esteem, self-empowerment, self-control, the emotional self, the compassionate self, self-deception, self-discipline, self-discovery, self-help, self-treatment, self-worth, self-doubt, self-sufficiency, self-reliance, self-regulation, self-coaching, self-love, self-healing, self-defeat, self-respect, self-confidence, the divided self, the authentic self, a separate self, self-promotion, the deluded self, the self absorbed, self-made, self-aware, self-acceptance, self-sabotage, self-destruction, self-hate, the haunted self, self-realization, self-centredness, self-forgiveness, the undefended self, the true self, the higher self, the original self, the spiritual self, self-motivation, the quantum self, self-interest, and on it goes.

At first glance, these ideas all seem like worthy, even noble pursuits. They do, however, promote a somewhat paradoxical conception of a person. For example, when someone undertakes self-empowerment, who or what is doing the empowering and who or what is being empowered? Presumably there is something we are calling the 'self' that is being empowered. Or is it the self that is doing the empowering? If the self is being empowered, how is that empowering happening?

It seems to make sense that whatever empowers something else must itself be a powerful thing since it is hard to imagine a power*less* entity *empowering* something else. So if we assume that the thing *doing* the empowering is itself empowered then, it must be the case that a part of the person travelling down the self-empowerment path is *already* empowered. Isn't that at least a little bit curious?

Who is My Self?

The idea central to all of these approaches seems to be that there is a 'self' that is some distance from a desired state and it is each individual's task to caress or coax or coerce or cuddle their 'self' into that more desired state. People who are successful in some way might be regarded as the ones who have most successfully tamed and harnessed their 'self'. Or perhaps it is the self that is doing the teaching or coaching to some other internal entity. Maybe the self is in the desired state and it is other things that need to be reined in. But what other things? And what is the 'self'?

Before embarking on any of these improvement adventures wouldn't it be wise to find out who is doing what to whom? If you are going to work on 'self-love', for example, shouldn't you at least know who or what is doing the loving and who or what is receiving it (and who decided 'you' needed to work on self-love in the first place?)? What about self-deceit? Who or what is doing the deceiving and who or what is being deceived? And why would some form of internal deceit be going on anyway?

All of these ideas, concepts, and approaches seem to be communicating the idea that there are at least two entities that comprise our being. There is something that does the acting and something that is acted upon. One of these we seem to have designated the 'self' and it has received the bulk of our attention. When we engage in self-talk, for example, there must be an inside talker and an inside listener.

So, if there are at least two entities involved in our ongoing meandering through life, shouldn't we be paying attention to both of them? When we are engaging in self-healing, for example, shouldn't we find out at least a little bit about the part that's doing the healing and the part that's being healed?

We would apply this same line of reasoning to any of the self-movements: self-sabotage, self-discovery, and so on. Currently, however, it seems that the 'self' is the one who gets all the attention. We wonder if the other entity might not get more than a little irked from time to time at being ignored and pushed around as completely as it is.

Perhaps, rather than describing our current time as the 'age of the self', it would be more accurate to say that we are living in the 'age of the bettered self' because most of the information available seems to be promoting the message that if you buy this book or take this course or watch this DVD or listen to this CD or do these daily exercises you will make your 'self' better than it was before. There are books, for example, offering to help you release your inner gifts or some other enchanting treat such as stepping out of your shadow and into your life.

Some other approaches take a paradoxical angle on it all and invite you to entertain the notion of a 'no-self'. Buddhism, for example, teaches the captivating idea of there not being a 'self' at all. At least, not in the way we currently think of ourselves. Adopting this point of view would eliminate problems of low (or high) self-esteem because there wouldn't be any self to be esteemed.

The age of the bettered self also incorporates concepts such as willpower, motivation, and regulation. Many problems of living are often attributed to insufficient quantities of willpower, low levels of motivation, or faulty regulatory processes. The idea seems to be that if the quantities can be restored, or the levels adjusted, or the processes fine-tuned, then the self will be functioning optimally. We touched on willpower in the last chapter and we'll now explore that, and other ideas more fully in the context of the programs that are offered to help with these things.

The Downside of Self-Control

Many self-improvement programs that are currently available either in groups, or alone, or with a therapist or coach, are designed to help people with motivation, willpower, or regulation. Various programs exhort people to try harder, think clearer, remain steadfast, and resist temptation. Techniques abound to help people correct faulty thinking, or create new life scripts, or develop new behaviors, or manage their emotions. Some strategies are taught from a similar stance to the Buddhist notion of 'no-self'. These strategies purport not to be about change at all. So, rather than changing troublesome thoughts, people are encouraged just to 'observe' their pesky imaginings from a distance. Instead of thinking you're a no-good, lousy piece of toe-cheese, now you can just observe yourself thinking you're a no-good lousy piece of toe-cheese. Changing perspective from thinking to observing actually does seem to be a change to us but that's a minor detail.

The common ground for all this different material seems to be the focus on creating a calm and pleasant place inside one's skull. Life is full, it seems, of internal dilemmas and struggles. Life is also pretty full of advice regarding what to do about these internal conflicts. We think of them as internal conflicts because they seem to be characterized by two (at least) components that are in opposition with each other. It's the internal opposition that creates misery and unhappiness. Some people might engage in self-destructive behaviors but not be bothered about that at all. Where botheration exists in the context of self-destruction, however, the simplest explanation is that it is arising from the tension between a part of the self that wants to destruct and a part that doesn't. One chap described having both a 'desire for oblivion' and a 'thirst for life'. It is not hard to imagine how an intense conflict might play out with these important and incompatible desires.

Actually, we've known about internal conflict for a very long time. Plato, for example, identified a 'reasoning' versus 'desiring' dilemma. Perhaps advice to help resolve these dilemmas has been with us for just as long. Current approaches, however, don't seem to recognize that what they are dealing with *is* internal conflict. In fact, from time to time some approaches seem to actually *increase* the conflict that exists. In order to understand the capabilities of any of these programs we think it's essential to have an accurate under-standing of how a person's misery is being generated. It is just such an accurate understanding, however, that is missing in all the guidance about how to live more harmoniously within your own skin. You may even question whether a functional explanation is necessary. It is certainly the case that many people receive a lot of psychological sustenance from the information that is currently available. It is also the case, however, that a great deal of people are not helped at all by this information. Some people in fact actually find things getting worse than they were before once they start tinkering with their inside goings-on.

Who Restoreth My Self

We don't want to rain on the self-improvement parade, or ruin anyone's party, but there are some important details left out of most explanations offering to introduce you to the you you always knew you could be. We are not suggesting that people who find happiness by following the advice they are offered are not really happy. We are suggesting, however, that they are not happy for the reasons that the advice-givers provide. Accurate reasons and functional explanations are important if the most effective and efficient self-improve-ment programs are to be devised. As we said before, when everything is proceeding swimmingly it doesn't really matter how you understand the situation or what you think is really happening. Once things start to go off the rails, however, your ability to correct these things and get them running smoothly again will depend on how precisely you understand what is happening.

If you believe that your presents at Christmas time are delivered by Santa Claus, you might spend the last few months leading up to Christmas being nice and not naughty, and you might even write a friendly note or two addressed to the North Pole. If your Christmas stocking does measure up to your expectations then all will be well and you might even try the same tactics next year. Suppose, however, that the sensible socks and unfashionable underwear that you retrieve from your stocking were not the things on your list. If you stick with the Santa explanation you might conclude that he didn't have his glasses on when he read your list. You might decide to start sending letters earlier next year in bigger print and try harder to be a picture of pleasantness all year round. If Santa is responsible for your Christmas bounty then this might well be successful and you could end up with what you want next year. If your explanation is inaccurate, however, you will be wasting time and energy. Once you discover that Granny May is really responsible for filling the stockings, your remediation strategies will change markedly. You might offer to carry Granny's shopping for her. You might leave notes where Granny can see them and you might even blurt out subtle hints when you are talking to her. Your strategies have a much greater chance of being successful once you have an accurate explanation of what is going on.

The same principles apply to the important issue of sorting out battles from within. The reorganizing system that we have already explained is an incredible restorative device that humans have been endowed with to reorganize our hardware when we are faced with intractable problems. The time we have already spent discussing the reorganization system was time well spent. It is the reorganization system that is the knight in shining armor when it comes to the resolution of internal conflict. The good part about our reorganization capacity is that even the most distressing turmoil can be resolved given the right conditions and sufficient time. It may be something of a drawback to this ability, however, that, because it works so well, almost any technique will seem successful if it's applied to enough people. It might be this fact that is behind the burgeoning panoply of remedies and self-improvement programs. As long as you don't do anything too drastic to prevent the body's own reorganization process from getting to work, then you are going to be successful with some people some of the time. When you are not successful with other people you can always put it down to the complexity of the problem, or that it wasn't the right time for the person, or that they had one of the 'treatment resistant' strains of the condition. What people rarely do is wonder if there was perhaps some shortcoming in their technique or their understanding of what is wrong and how they are fixing it.

What most self-improvement programs and protocols leave out of their resource kit is a plausible explanation of how a distressing condition changes into a contented one. How does an irrational thought morph into a rational one? How does a dysfunctional assumption transmogrify into a functional one? How do you step back and observe those nasty little thoughts lazily wandering through your consciousness until they drift out of sight. When you are able to better regulate your emotions, just what exactly has happened to perk up your regulatory machinery? There's an unspoken, unacknowledged, yet essential process that occurs within every approach, every time it is successful.

A lack of awareness of this approach and a lack of under-standing of the functional manifestation of psychological distress have paved the way for a kaleidoscope of approaches and treatments. Worse than the promulgation of different packages, however, is the fact some people aren't being helped at all, some people are getting worse, and even the people who are helped are being helped serendipitously. In the next chapter we will look at an approach to reducing psychological distress through an understanding of its ultimate cause — conflict — and the process by which it is reduced — reorgan-ization. Having introduced the mechanics of the reorganization system we'll discuss its practical importance in reducing psychological distress.

Chapter 8

Resolving Conflict: Going Up a Level

So far we have discussed how common as well as how devastating conflict can be. The ubiquity of conflict is vastly underestimated. From the perspective of control theory, any choice situation is essentially a conflict. Choosing between the checked shirt or the striped shirt in order to clinch the important business deal and choosing between a candlelit dinner at a favorite restaurant or a moonlit stroll on the pier to pop the question are both conflict situations. They might not seem like it at first but the very fact that a choice is required means that there are different states a variable can be in but only one state is possible for that one occasion. The variable of appearance can only be in one state (checked or striped) when the contract is being signed and the romantic atmosphere variable can only be in one state (soft lighting, hushed tones, and fine food, or waves crashing, glistening water, and balmy breeze) when the crucial question is being delivered.

If all choices are really conflicts in disguise then the mundaneness of conflict quickly becomes apparent. What also becomes very obvious is how good controlling people are at resolving conflict most of the time. We generally don't stand immobilized at the front of the queue in the cinema unable to choose between the comedy or the thriller. Nor do we remain stuck indefinitely at the restaurant unable to tell the waitress that we want the slow cooked partridge breast instead of the poached Wagyu beef.

Dealing with Everyday Conflicts

Clearly, most people don't spend most of their time debilitated by either intra- or inter-personal conflict. We are generally able to negotiate choices within a time frame that causes no more than a blip in the everyday processes of daily life. It is certainly true that some people do, on occasion, experience chronic and incapacitating conflict but given how common conflict is, it must be the case that effective and efficient ways of resolving conflict exist. Unresolved conflict would spell big trouble for the continued survival of both an individual and a group. Conflict effectively removes the ability to be in control. The long-term effects can be vacillation, immobilization, being pushed around by environmental circumstances, and sudden and severe rebound effects where individuals can find themselves engaging in unproductive behaviors excessively. For example, in Chapter 6 we described the way in which dieting behavior can result in periods of deprivation on the one hand and gorging feasts on the other.

Conflict is particularly pernicious because it occupies so much of a person's attention and energy. People in conflict spend an enormous amount of time worrying or otherwise thinking about different aspects of the conflict. They can also expend considerable personal resources 'making' themselves behave in particular ways (such as pushing themselves to go out in public despite their fear of critical scrutiny), or 'forcing' themselves to do certain things (such as ignoring their desire to stay in bed and nagging themselves to get on with things — have a shower, and get ready for work), or trying hard to resist urges and live productively (such as heading straight home without stopping off at the liquor store).

While people can devote a great deal of time and effort to coping with various conflicts, we don't consider a life spent forcing oneself to behave in particular ways to be the ideal solution. People who continually need support and encouragement to stay on the 'straight and narrow' have not resolved their conflicts. How one copes with one's conflict is, ultimately, a personal decision, but our optimistic view is that conflicts can always be resolved satisfactorily. It is not necessary to spend a lifetime burdened by the shackles of conflict. Spending the span of one's life yoked to a particular routine or course of action is a hard way to live. Our reorganization system, as a robust and indefatigable learning mechanism is, quite literally, a lifeline for those who seek a clearer, more relaxed, and pleasurable existence.

One of the difficulties with resolving conflict is that many of the useful learning strategies that we've acquired along the way such as *brainstorming* and *cost-benefit analysis* will be perfectly useless when it comes to conflict. When a conflict sets in there is simply no logical way to think yourself out of it. There is no rational way that you can have both social approval and doing things your own way at the same time. It is impossible to refuse food and eat food simultaneously. What is needed, therefore, is some novel solution. Some approach or mechanism is required that can create something that wasn't there before. Running through lists of alternatives that are already in your repertoire of resources won't help. At least, if they could help, they would have helped long before the conflict became chronic.

Reorganization and Conflict Resolution

Essentially then, what is necessary is a way of learning that does not itself need to be learned. That sentence might be a bit confusing so we'll unpack it a little. One of the problems with relying on strategies such as brainstorming or cost-benefit analysis is that these strategies themselves had to be learned. Little babies are not born with the ability to weigh up the pros and cons of a given situation and select between the weighted options. So let's say you learned about the advantages of cost-benefit analysis when you were 14. If this problem-solving approach was the ideal way to solve conflicts that means that any conflict you developed when you were 8 would have to stick around for another 6 years until you developed the skills to get rid of it. And if you were holidaying with your family in Hawaii when they taught cost-benefit analysis? You might never learn how to deal with conflicts at all.

Fortunately, however, we have a powerful and fundamental learning mechanism that has been with us since before we were born. Anyone who has spent any time with babies or young children will be able to appreciate the tremendous capacity for learning that exists right from the start. Before even the simplest learning occurs, the *ability* to learn is there. This learning mechanism is the reorganization system discussed in Chapter 5. As you may recall, when controlling goes wrong and error persists, our reorganization mechanism begins making random changes to the control hierarchy. When one of these random changes reduces the error, that change persists. If the error is not reduced, then another change soon occurs. So, when things aren't right, reorganization will get things humming again given the opportunity.

If you can recall a time when you have been particularly stressed about something, you might be able to remember solutions and ideas running through your mind. Some of these ideas might have seemed crazy or preposterous but some might also have seemed feasible. Eventually, you might have even had a 'light bulb' or 'Aha!' moment when something occurred to you that you hadn't seen before. Once it occurred to you, you might even have found yourself wondering how you could have not seen something so obvious. This may very well be the experience of reorganization.

So reorganization is the mechanism that can do what is required to resolve conflict. A learning mechanism that is so fundamental that it is there from the beginning. It's a learning process that does not need to be learned itself, and it is robust and flexible enough to cover a wide range of situations, circumstances, contexts, and abilities. The other aspect to reorganization is that it is pretty much automatic. We can't arbitrarily decide to reorganize. If we could, it wouldn't exactly be a random trial and error process would it? The starting and stopping of reorganization is determined by error.

Directing Reorganization

With a powerful learning mechanism like this operating on auto-pilot in our heads it would have to be pretty important to make sure that only the systems that weren't operating optimally were tinkered with. It would be a fairly awful state of affairs to wake up one morning and discover that areas of your life you'd been perfectly satisfied with were now viewed from a different perspective. Fortunately, reorganization seems to only work in the general area it is needed. We say the 'general area' here because sometimes reorganization can be occurring in roughly the right vicinity without yet having picked exactly the best spot to work its magic.

Another feature of our experience that seems to be related to learning and reorganization is consciousness. We first mentioned consciousness in Chapter 5. It is relevant again in this part of the discussion. It is hard to imagine learning something or reorganizing a new perspective without being conscious of this change in some way. One only has to watch a young baby learning to reach for a toy to appreciate the tremendous amount of consciousness and focus that seems to be involved. Similarly, one doesn't seem to be able to acquire the ability to hit a backhand topspin lob without some attention to detail. It is certainly the case that when one is in conflict, consciousness is involved as well. One truism that might apply to conflict is that when people are in conflict they know about it. At the very least, they know they are bothered, perturbed, or distressed. People can, in fact, become consumed by conflict. At least they can become consumed by part of the conflict. We have already discussed the fact that there are two incompatible goals involved in all conflicts. Well, these conflicted goals weren't always in conflict but they were always there for a reason. Those particular goals are being used to achieve other goals and are also influencing more instrumental goals at the same time. A goal to wear the striped shirt, for example, is set in order to help achieve a certain impression at work. In order to achieve the goal of wearing the striped shirt a number of simpler goals need to be set such as walking to the wardrobe, ironing the shirt, buttoning it up, and so on. Quite a few other goals, therefore, are potentially implicated in any conflict.

From this perspective, consciousness can be both a blessing and a curse. Consciousness is a blessing because it indicates what part of the conflict the person is focusing on and it also suggests where reorganization is going about its business at the present time. It is a curse, however, because, by focusing on the incompatible goals, consciousness seems to keep reorganization occupied at the level of incompatible goals. In fact it often seems to be the case that people are not even conscious of both sides of a conflict. People might be conscious of how much they want other people to like them but they might not be completely conscious that it is also simultaneously important to them to speak their mind. Or they might be conscious of how important it is for them to feel hungry and look svelte, or how strongly they want to avoid the scrutiny of others, but they might not be so in touch with their desire to eat what they like or to experience the enjoyment of social gatherings.

If reorganization works on whatever area is in consciousness then most of the time reorganization will be working its trial and error charms on the incompatible goals. Unfortunately, reorganization will not have any ultimate effect on the conflict by focusing on the disagreeing goals. It is not those goals that need to be reorganized but the higher level they are serving. Reorganization, therefore, will effectively solve the conflict when it is directed to the higher level goals that the two conflicted goals are attempting to satisfy.

When you think about it, that seems to be pretty much the way that any conflict get resolved. The internal conversation about which shirt to wear might go something like this:

> *Should I wear the striped shirt or the checked shirt?*
>
> *I really like the striped shirt.*
>
> *I like the checked shirt too.*
>
> *The colors in the striped shirt match my best trousers.*
>
> *But I've got a neat tie that looks great with the checked shirt.*
>
> *Hmmm maybe the stripes. Yep, the stripes.*

Actually, I think I should go with the checks.

*Stripes, checks, stripes, checks, stripes, checks –
Darn! Why do I always do this?*

*Wait a minute! It's easy. The checks are a bit
more casual and the stripes look more serious —
this is an important contract. I want them to
take me seriously. So the stripes it is.*

Cool!

The war of the shirts thus continued until the career-minded gent realized that what he was after was a serious look. The goal that was more important than wearing stripes or checks was the goal of being taken seriously. Once his consciousness popped up there, the conflict no longer existed. If you hear people talk about their struggles or their dilemmas they will almost always tell you about incompatible goals or even just one goal that they can't seem to achieve. For as long as they stay paying attention to these conflicted goals, their conflict will persist. Ironically, their consciousness has to turn away from the conflict to the place the conflict is coming from in order to genuinely and thoroughly remove the conflict. Going to the source is the important part.

So when people are in conflict, it isn't the case that their reorganization mechanism has abandoned them or is faulty. It is simply occurring in the wrong place. Wrong in the sense that reorganization here will have no ultimate impact on the conflict. It's a bit like noticing a red light on the dashboard of your car and fixing the problem by covering up the red light with a sticking plaster. That will stop you seeing the redness of the light but it won't solve the problem. When there is error being experienced, reorganization will be at work — it's just that sometimes it is running on the spot by being asked to work in a place where it can't have any effect.

Looking Up to Solve Conflicts

This simple principle — of becoming conscious of the higher level goals involved in conflicts — seems to be at the heart of most effective therapies. Within the rationale of just about any psychological therapy there is some mention of helping a person become more fully conscious of the nature of their problems. The language used to describe this by different therapies can vary, and the methods used can differ enormously, but the general purpose seems to be the same.

In Chapter 5 we first mentioned a therapy based on PCT called the Method of Levels (MOL). MOL[1] focuses entirely on helping people shift their consciousness to the important goals that underpin the conflict being experienced. It is accepted as given that when people are in conflict they don't know what this more valued goal is. If they did know what it was that would suggest that they were conscious of it in some way and reorganization would probably already have started working on it. So MOL is a process of exploration where neither the therapist nor the client knows what lies ahead or what will be illuminated by the client's consciousness. The exploration continues for as long as the client needs it to until the important goal is found and the conflict disappears.

It might sound a bit mysterious and spooky to discuss directing consciousness to unidentified goals but, in practice, it's quite straightforward to redirect someone's attention. If we were currently having a conversation with you and we suddenly pointed in your direction and said 'Oh my gosh, what's that big, hairy spider on your shoulder?' then your attention would probably shift from the engaging and charming conversation we were having to the alleged eight-legged intruder perched beside your collar. If consciousness is connected to error, then the key to directing consciousness is to try and create some error in the place you want consciousness to go. With unresolved conflict you don't know exactly where you want consciousness to land but you know the direction in which you want it to go. You want it to go higher or deeper, to more important reasons for what people are doing. Fortunately, it has proven to be the case that if you start people talking about the problem they are currently experiencing they will give clues, without really realizing it, as to where these next goals might be. The essence of MOL is to pick up on these clues and to follow them.

Actually, it's a funny thing about consciousness and experience. As we mentioned in Chapter 5, consciousness isn't actually needed for control at all. Cruise control systems in cars control perfectly well without ever being conscious. We live our lives only ever being conscious of the perceptual signals of a tiny proportion of the total set of control systems that make up who we are. We are not conscious of all of our controlling but we go about controlling anyway. Even when we are not conscious of controlling we still carry on our controlling business.

When we have the experience of a thought 'popping' into our mind, therefore, it's much more likely to be the case that our mind (or at least consciousness) popped over to the thought in question. If that's what happened, it might also be the case that when someone is experiencing racing thoughts it is actually their consciousness that is racing from one place to another. Similarly when someone is 'stuck' on a thought and has the same thing going over and over in their mind, it might be consciousness that is actually fixated on the one spot for the time being. Sometimes people describe having a song in their head that they can't get out. Again, what seems to be a more accurate explanation of this situation is that consciousness is picking out a particular spot in the person's tapestry of experience and won't budge. For some reason (and it may be the reason that's the key) consciousness is especially attracted to that little tune — out of all the melodies you have in your repertoire — at that particular time.

Conscious of Consciousness

There is still no consensus on what consciousness actually is or its purpose but it does seem to be the case that it can move rapidly around throughout our experiential world. As with reorganization it doesn't seem to be the case that consciousness is entirely 'controlled'. We just seem to become conscious of different things. Sometimes the environment affects what we are conscious of and sometimes there doesn't seem to be any environmental occurrence. However it works, it seems to be the case that we are always 'on' and we are always conscious. Sometimes we're not even conscious that we're conscious but we're still conscious nevertheless. Have you ever had the experience of driving somewhere and getting to the destination and not being able to remember all that you did on the trip? We described a similar driving experience in Chapter 5. It does not seem very contentious to assume that since you arrived safely, you probably kept the car on the road and successfully negotiated traffic lights, pedestrians, corners, and so on; you were in control of the car. But you probably also ran into little conflicts along the way as well: Should I try to make the light or stop? Take the high road or the low one? Negotiating all of those little conflicts must have required some degree of consciousness.

So we are conscious even when we are 'not conscious' and we are controlling even when we are not conscious of our controlling. In fact, it might even be more precise to say that control is not something we *do*, it is something we *are*. It is certainly the case that we can feel 'in control' and we can plan and imagine and set goals about how we would like things to be. All of these experiences though are just part of the automatic, natural, and elegantly beautiful process of control. Control is never something we can step outside of and simply watch unfold — unless you are watching your cruise control system control your car's speed.

It might not be possible to prevent conflicts from occurring but it is certainly possible to develop a mindset of flexible consciousness. Whenever you get stuck on something, if you listen to the chatter of your mind (all of it), and focus on the 'why' of your distress, you may be able to reorganize yourself to a more contented state of mind. Sometimes, even saying out loud the thoughts you are having on the inside can be helpful. For reasons that are not entirely obvious yet, there seems to be something very useful in saying out loud and hearing back through your own ears the thoughts you have been running on internal dialogue only. More importantly, if you can catch any thoughts you are having *about* the words you hear yourself saying you might just have found the 'X' that marks the spot for a useful reorganization.

Conflicts will persist for as long as we remain unconscious of the significant higher level goal underpinning the two incompatible alternatives we are currently stuck with. For many conflicts we quickly and effortlessly shift our attention to the higher priority and move forward having made the most appropriate choice. Other conflicts are less straightforward and can result in chronic distress and despair. Fortunately, it is not necessary to spend a lifetime riddled with the uncertainty, indecision, and misery of chronic conflict. Reorganization is a fundamental learning process that will find a way out of the conflict if it is helped to look in the right place. By directing the gaze of consciousness towards those lofty places in our mind where we dare to dream and plot a course for ourselves of a life worth living we will be giving reorganization the best chance it has of dissolving the conflict. And who knows? We might even find that the life worth living is the one we have just discovered.

Chapter 9

Freedom and Control

Freedom may be just another word for 'nothin' left to lose' but it is also a word for something people seem to cherish, to the point where they are willing to risk, and often to give, their lives to achieve or maintain it. For many, perhaps most, freedom is essential to life, so that life without freedom is simply not worth living. So what is freedom and why do we treasure it so? Whatever freedom is it is intimately tied up with the concept of control. For example, most dictionaries include this as one of its main definitions of freedom: 'exemption from external control, interference, regulation, etc.' According to the dictionary then, 'freedom' means freedom from being controlled. But what is it that we are free to do when we are not being controlled? The answer is that we are free to do what we want. And as we have seen, PCT shows us that doing what we want means being in control. So according to PCT, freedom is just another word for *being in control*.

You Say You Want a Revolution

By defining freedom as 'being in control' we can use our understanding of the nature of controlling people to analyze freedom from a PCT perspective. This is useful because PCT explains not only how control works (when it works) but also why it doesn't (when it doesn't). In other words, PCT can explain what makes us free 'in control') and what gets in the way of our freedom (keeping us from being 'in control'). To see how such an analysis works let's look at a very simple example of controlling: opening the door. According to PCT, this simple behavior involves acting to bring your perception of the door to the state 'open', which is specified by a reference signal in your brain. The actions that bring the perception to the reference state are driven by error signals created by any discrepancy between the current and reference state of the door. The error signals must drive actions that reduce those error signals. If the door is closed, the error signal must drive actions, such as turning the handle and pushing on the door, that open the door and eliminate the error that caused those very actions. You successfully control for opening the door when error drives your actions so as to bring your perception of the state of the door to the reference state: an open door.

We usually have no problem opening a door — we just 'do it' without even thinking about it. This is what it feels like to be in control. You produce the perception you want (an open door in this case) seemingly without effort. You may not perceive you are in control, in fact you probably won't think about control at all. People don't normally think to themselves as they are opening a door 'Here I am being in control and opening the door' — they just go about their controlling ways and get the door to the state they want it to be in. This is what freedom feels like too. Freedom is effortlessly getting what you want. It is being in control. When we are controlling successfully we aren't thinking about being free or wanting to be free; we are free. We become aware of the limitations of our freedom when we start to lose control. When we turn the knob and the knob doesn't move, we feel like we have lost control. Losing control is like losing our freedom — we are suddenly no longer free to get what we want. PCT shows us that there are three main ways that control (and thus freedom) can fail: *overwhelming disturbance, ignorance,* and *conflict.*

Overwhelming Disturbance

Control involves acting against disturbances as necessary in order to bring a perception to a reference state. When you are opening a door, disturbances are things such as friction and mechanical connections that determine how much force you have to use to turn the knob or how hard you have to pull on the knob to open a particular door. The turning and pulling forces you exert are the actions that get the door open. You can't open doors using the exact same actions every time. The same force might be too little to get some doors open and too much for others. You control for getting a door open by automatically generating just the right forces to get the door open. You are usually unconscious of the variations in the forces you use to get doors open — you just open the door. But sometimes the door requires a great deal of force and then you might notice that you are producing an unusual action to get the door open. But if you can produce enough force to open the door then the fact that you have to use an unusual amount of force to open it is just an annoyance. But suppose that you are simply unable to generate enough force to open the door at all. In this case, there is a disturbance — perhaps a rusted joint or an obstruction in the lock — that you simply can't overcome with any amount of force. This is an overwhelming disturbance and it has prevented you from getting what you want. Because there is an overwhelming disturbance you are not free.

Overwhelming disturbances are natural events that prevent control simply because we don't have the resources available to overcome them. Natural phenomena such as hurricanes, earthquakes, floods, bushfires, tornados, etc. are examples of what are often overwhelming disturbances to people's ability to control for shelter, food, and comfort. When these natural phenomena deprive people of the ability to control, they are depriving them of their freedom. A person is not free to live in their house once it has been leveled by an earthquake or tornado. Similarly, it doesn't matter how tightly you grip the steering wheel while you're driving in a hurricane — the muscular forces you are able to produce will be ineffectual and puny compared to the overwhelming, magnificently powerful forces of the wind. You can't rollerskate in a buffalo herd. It's that kind of thing. So, one impediment to freedom is the possibility of overwhelming disturbance.

The only way to maintain one's freedom (ability to control) in the face of the possibility of overwhelming disturbance is to prepare, as best as one can, for the possibility of such disturbances. Investing in disaster preparedness is, thus, an investment in freedom.

Ignorance

In order to be able to do anything — to be in control — you have to have built the control systems that can do this controlling. This means you have to have built control systems that know what perceptions to control, what references to set for those perceptions, and what actions to take in order to maintain those perceptions in their reference states, protected from disturbances. For example, in order to be able to catch a baseball you have to know what visual perception to control, what the goal states of those perceptions should be, and what to do when what you are perceiving doesn't match those references. If you haven't built up these control systems you are ignorant of how to control for catching a ball. Thus, ignorance deprives you of the freedom to do what you want (in this case, to catch baseballs).

Travelling to other countries can provide good examples of the loss of control through ignorance. Though these experiences are often amusing and don't last for very long they are excellent illustrations of what can happen without having developed the appropriate control systems. It's amazing how many different ways there can be to flush a toilet or turn a tap on in a bathroom. Some taps have little sensors that come on automatically when you wave your hands near them. Other taps have little buttons that need to be pushed to make the water appear. Not knowing how the particular taps you are standing in front of work, means you won't be able to control as effortlessly as you normally do.

A few years ago some friends of ours arrived in Bolivia for a holiday. As their host picked them up at the airport he explained that an emergency had just occurred which meant he would need to be out of town for a few days. He had packed the house with food so he was sure they would be well catered for until he returned. Nothing untoward happened in his absence but there were many hilarious situations of trying to figure out what was in a particular can of food or going to the local shop and not knowing how to ask for what they wanted. Again, control was much less automatic and much more restricted than it would have been if our friends were back in their home town. They were not keen to wander too far from where they were staying, for example, because they couldn't read any of the signs and didn't know if they would be able to make their way back.

The way to maintain one's freedom in the face of ignorance is through education. Investment in education is, thus, another investment in freedom.

Conflict

If freedom is being in control then we have already discussed the most common impediment to freedom: conflict. Both kinds of conflict — intrapersonal and interpersonal — are impediments to control. But the people who seem to scream the loudest about maintaining their freedom are protesting the kind of conflict that occurs when other people get in the way of their controlling — interpersonal conflict. What many of these people see as the main impediment to their freedom is the government. Yet the government is just other controlling people who are trying to enforce the rules of society. To enforce these rules, government people sometimes have to 'push back' against the people who they perceive to be not following the rules. This deprives the controlling people who are being 'enforced against' of their ability to do what they want — to control — and, therefore, these people feel like they are being deprived of their freedom.

People who see the government as an 'oppressor' are being deprived of their freedom in the same way that a person who wants to open a door is being deprived of their freedom when they find that someone on the other side of the door is trying to keep it closed. The freedom to open the door — to control it — is being denied by interpersonal conflict with another controlling person.

Some people imagine that they would be truly free if there were no government there to push back against them. This might be true if people could do all their own controlling without ever interfering with the controlling done by others. But the fact is that people are always 'stepping on each other's toes' (so to speak) even in situations where there is no government at all, such as in private interpersonal interactions. In the larger society there are also people who seem to want to control for things that interfere with the controlling done by other people. There is always a bad actor around. That's probably one reason why governments were developed in the first place — to protect everyone from the occasional bad actor. But there are other reasons for having a government. People's ability to control is enhanced enormously when they coordinate their controlling. Coordination requires making agreements — contracts — regarding who will do what, when, and for what return. These contracts work only if everyone cooperates and they fail if there are dubious actors who enter such contracts in bad faith. Again, governments are created to enforce these cooperative contracts.

So governments are created by (and made up of) controlling people as a means of helping them control better, by creating the rules for coordinated, non-conflicting interaction between controlling people. In order to maintain this well-coordinated, conflict-free interaction (society), some of the people who make up the government have to enforce the rules, which often puts them in conflict with people who either don't agree on what the rules are, or who don't want to follow the rules, period. So once again we confront a paradox of controlling people — in order to be in control (free) people have to allow themselves to be controlled (to play by the rules of society). This is actually the paradox that all societies have to confront. How to organize themselves so that each individual is best able to control their own life without giving up too much control to the powers that be. The powers that be are those people (or a small subset of them, if we are talking about a dictatorship) who enforce the rules that are implemented to reduce interpersonal conflict. By enforcing these rules, however, the powers that be are also creating interpersonal conflict to some extent. So in the process of enforcing the rules that increase personal freedom, the government (in the form of the people who make it up) is seen as a force that con-strains freedom.

So freedom cannot be achieved by abolishing the govern-ment. The result would be anarchy where the strong — the best controllers — will be free to deprive the weak (through conflict) of their freedom — their ability to control. And of course freedom cannot be achieved by making the government all powerful so that the strong and the weak are controlled equally by absolute rule (a mega controller perhaps?). In this case the mega-controller is the only one who feels free. The only solution is the one that mankind has been working on for thousands of years. A government that is somehow account-able for whatever enforcement it does. The liberal democracies of today are probably getting close to the best we can do. But we can always keep working toward improving things if we keep in mind that the goal is for every member of society to be in control of their lives. The best society is one where everyone is in control. That means a society without the main sources of loss of control: poverty (as an overwhelming disturbance) ignorance, and minimal conflict.

Freedom to Control

Interpersonal conflict is not the only kind of conflict that deprives people of their freedom. Intrapersonal conflict also deprives us of our freedom since it reduces or eliminates our ability to control. A controlling person who is caught in a net of intrapersonal conflicts is not free to do as they please. The person whose conflict involves controlling for incompatible perceptions, such as pleasing one's parents by staying home and studying and pleasing oneself by going out to meet one's boy or girlfriend is not free to do as they please. What they please to do is two incompatible things; staying home to study and going out on a date. The person who wants to do both these things is free to do neither because it is physically impossible to be in two different places at the same time. A person in conflict is free to control either of the perceptions involved in the conflict, but not both at the same time. Once again we confront the paradox of controlling people — controlling (two incompatible things at the same time) leads to loss of control. Freedom leads to loss of freedom.

The way to free one's self from the debilitating effects of conflict is to 'reorganize' one's controlling so that the conflict no longer exists. This reorganization is often as easy as realizing that it is possible to control for both perceptions involved in the conflict, just not at the same time. So reorganization of the study/date conflict may be as simple as realizing that it is possible to please the parents by studying and then going out on a date afterwards. In this case, freedom comes from disciplining your own controlling. As in the case of interpersonal conflict, freedom (in the sense of the ability to control what you want) comes from giving up some freedom (the freedom to control for two perceptions at the same time).

If freedom, then, is another word for 'being in control', it is in these three simple words 'being in control' that the key to expanding our freedom lies. It might be stating the obvious, but there are two parts to being in control — wanting and doing. The doing is created by the wanting — or, to be more precise, the doing is created by the difference between what you currently want and what you've currently got. If you really want a red Lamborghini but each time you look in your garage you see a white Toyota Corolla, then there will be a big difference between 'want' and 'got'. In this sense you are not free to drive the car that you want. But (and it's a big but), if you *wanted* a white Toyota Corolla, life would be sweet.

So our freedoms at any particular time, and in any given situation, are largely determined by the goals we set ourselves.

It might very well be the case that nothing is good or bad but wanting makes it so. If we want to spend a day at the beach soaking up the sun then a weather forecast for rain and showers will severely restrict our freedom. If, however, we want our garden, rather than our skin, to get the soaking it needs, then we'll be getting just what we want. Whether the weather is good or bad depends on what we want to do. This is another example of the idea of relativity that we mentioned in Chapter 4. In a very real sense we fence ourselves in by the boundaries and walls and limits we set ourselves in our mind by the goals we pursue.

Without really realizing it, goals are both limiting and liberating. Deciding to pursue one goal necessarily means you can't pursue other goals simultaneously. This is precisely the reason that conflict arises. Ironically, determining that you want to spend your holidays in the south of France *immediately* restricts your freedom! You won't be free, for example, to enjoy the beautiful sights of Capetown. If exploring the south of France, however, is really what you want to do, you won't even notice this deprivation of your liberties. You'll be doing what you want — you will be in control. If someone pointed out to you that, by securing your cottage in that quaint Provence village you had just denied yourself the opportunity to visit the Two Oceans Aquarium at the V&A Waterfront in Capetown, you might think that was a little odd. You might even reply with something like 'But I don't want to go to Capetown'. It won't feel to you like you have just limited your choices. It will feel like you are doing what you want. You will feel free.

Our stance, based on a PCT understanding of human nature, is that being free means doing what you want. And doing what you want is defined by the 'want'. This is where the relativity comes in. If what you want most of all is to spend a night in your pajamas curled up in front of the television, then having your friends phone up to ask you out will be an imposition on your freedom. If, on the other hand, you want to be out in the nightlife meeting new people and having a wild time, then spending another night on your own in front of mind-numbing television shows might feel like being in prison.

Freedom through Consciousness Raising

At the end of the day, it's all down to us and what we want. Fortunately, we want lots of things, and having the flexibility to shift our consciousness to the higher, more valued, and perhaps more abstract goals will help to expand our freedom in any given situation. The more specific and particular your goals are in any given situation the greater the likelihood that your freedom will be restricted. If, for example, your plans for the perfect night are to be eating a particular meal at a particular table at a particular restaurant at a particular time with a particular someone, it will be very easy for the perfectness of this plan to go awry. Maybe they'll have run out of your favorite meal, or that table is reserved for another booking, or the restaurant is closed for renovations, or any one of a number of life's little speed bumps could occur. If, however, your perfect evening just means spending time in the company of someone you are fond of then it will be much easier for your night to measure up.

It is a bit like hitting a target. If the only place on the target you have your focus is the teensy spot in the middle then you will probably miss more than you will hit. If just landing on the target at all, however, is what you want then you will find it much easier to hit the mark. This isn't about dropping standards or accepting second best. It's about the specificity of our goals. It turns out that specific goals are connected to more abstract and more important goals. Whenever you are pursuing a specific goal and you feel your freedom shrinking, if you can begin to think about the more important, more general goals that are hovering overhead you will have a good shot at peeling back the constraints. This was the point we were making in Chapter 4 regarding the fact that we are not really free to set goals about absolutely anything at all. Our goals at a particular level in the hierarchy are set by systems at the level above, and goals at this level are set by systems at the level above it. In a sense, all goals are set relative to our highest level goals of being who we want to be and living the life we want to live. By keeping our consciousness aimed at these highest levels we will be as free and in control as we can be.

We have already mentioned the Method of Levels (MOL). It's relevant again here. The chief role of MOL is to help people to step up to the rooftops of their minds so they can survey the scene from a loftier vantage point. As it's explained in the song by the same name, events and situations can take on new meanings and seem very different when viewed 'from a distance'. It's perhaps not surprising that 'flexibility' is a synonym for 'freedom'. Having the flexibility to take the elevator all the way to the top, and spending a while taking in the scene from up above, will go a long way to helping people achieve the sense of freedom that is important to them.

This doesn't mean, necessarily, that we should accept intolerable circumstances and unacceptable situations. It certainly doesn't mean that we shouldn't fight for what we believe in. At the pinnacle of our being, however, we will have a much better sense of the battles that are worth fighting for. We will know with clarity and determination what is important to us, and we will also be more certain of the things that can fall by the wayside. We will understand with feeling and commitment the personal meaning of a life worth living and we will have a much better sense of the path we need to take to get there. We will be able to see the forest *and* the trees and we will understand with smug contentment who we are and what we are here for.

We don't have to stay up there forever either. But when we do descend into the thick of it once more we will have a confident spring in our step and will be able to engage in the daily 'busy-ness' of life knowing there is our own private sanctuary waiting for us whenever we need it. Our chief freedom then may be the freedom to navigate the territories of our mind to minimize conflicts and expand control. Being aware of what control is, how it works, and our own controlling nature might help us all to bump along together more harmoniously and to share in the task of seeking ways to get what we want without interfering with what other people want. In our final chapter we will apply our understanding of controlling people to see how we might go about building such a world — a world worth the trouble of trying to make it better.

Chapter 10

Living With Our Own Controlling Nature

Here we are now at the end of the book. Well, almost at the end. In this final chapter we'll draw together the points and lessons we've outlined in the previous chapters to paint a picture of what it all means from a PCT perspective. We'll cover previous ground and possibly repeat things we've said before. Our aim here is to provide a sketch of what a PCT world might be and whether it would be a world worth the trouble. The creator of PCT, Bill Powers, gives us a hint:

> The childhood of the human race is far from
> over. We have a long way to go before most
> people will understand that what they do for
> others is just as important to their well-being as
> what they do for themselves.[1]

Carrots and Sticks

Building a 'world worth the trouble' seems like a formidably daunting prospect but, actually, it is not that difficult. The difficulty is that we have been working with the wrong blueprint for a long time. The people who have been telling us how to build a better world have mostly been reading out of the 'carrots and sticks' manual.[2] This is the manual that was created from the technology that gave us control of behavior by the 'contingencies of reinforcement' that was discussed in Chapter 6. It's the manual that tells us how to make the world better by getting people to behave 'properly'. But that is the wrong book. We don't need to be told to control other people because we are controlling people by nature. What we need is the manual that tells us why our inclination to control other people is the reason why we so often see people behaving in the 'wrong way'. We need the manual that tells us about the problems created by our own controlling nature and that of the people we are inclined to control.

With an appreciation of the nature of people as controllers, things become easier to fathom. Knowing about our controlling nature even helps us better understand things like carrots and sticks. The basic situation with carrots is that the people with the carrots will use them to try and make other people do what they want them to do. And the carrot-less people will do what the carrot holders want them to do in order to get the carrots. So, in a sense, the carrot-holders are seen more as carrot-dispensers by those whose carrot supply needs replenishing.

In order for those with the carrots to continue to be able to control the other people, however, they have to make sure that those other people continue to want the carrots and have no other way of getting them except by doing what they 'should'. To do this, the carrot-lords have to give people carrots for doing what has been required of them, but they can only give them just enough carrots to satisfy them for now. The carrots will only keep working if the carrot-wanters remain, for the most part, carrot-deprived. Using rewards to control other people only ever works for those people who are in reward-deprived states. Now and then this fact about how rewards work might give you reason to pause, and question whether keeping people deprived of the things they want is conducive to long-term, harmonious social relationships.

To hold people in a carrot-deficient state means you have to be the sole carrot-merchant in the neighborhood. If there is another supply, then the carrot-seekers might just go elsewhere for their carrots, and you will have lost whatever control you had over them. Also, what you are asking them to do must not inconvenience or irritate them too much; otherwise, they might provide you with some sage advice about alternative uses for your carrots. And more than anything, the carrot has to be a carrot that the person to be controlled wants. If you're only dealing in Majestic Red carrots, but the person in your sights really wants a steady supply of Chantenays, then your efforts at control will be less than perfect.

We could do the same analysis for sticks that we have just done with carrots but you probably get the idea. By reading from a control manual, we can understand the trade in carrots as a simple transaction where the carrot provider is controlling the carrot receiver by producing desired carrots under certain conditions. At the same time, the carrot receiver is controlling the carrot provider by producing desired actions under certain conditions.

Is a carrots and sticks world one that is worth the trouble? Perhaps if carrots and sticks are understood from the control side of the fence things won't seem so bad. It is still not a great way to treat other people, but if everyone knows the score, then the interaction becomes more transparent, more honest. This increase in understanding and honesty also provides scope for a greater range of options. When you change the position from which things are being viewed, new possibilities become apparent. If you have just mown the front lawn, you can stand on the lawn and inspect your work, or, you could climb the stairs to the landing for a better view. We think the control manual helps us climb the stairs to the landing for a better view.

When a better view of the mechanics of carrot-based interactions is possible, you can get a sense of why this form of social exchange is never entirely satisfactory for any length of time with very many people. Sooner or later, the people being 'carrotted' might change their minds about the number of carrots they are getting, or what they are being required to do to get carrots. They might start to get a little niggly sense that they are not really doing what they want or, at least, not doing all of what they want. Or, alternatively, the people handing out the carrots might form the idea that they can make their carrots go further. The carroters might insist that people now do more work for fewer carrots. Whichever way it goes, the carrot status quo never seems to persist for very long. Having a sense of the controlling nature of us all allows us to appreciate why this might be so.

We once knew of a 10-year-old boy whose teacher decided to introduce a token economy to the class. The students were told that when they acted in particular ways, such as completing work and following instructions, they would receive tokens from the teacher. The students could then trade their tokens for desirable things such as free time or access to the class computer. Lachlan decided not to spend any of the tokens he was given so, after a few weeks, he had accumulated more tokens than the teacher had in stock. Then, the enterprising young chap started to give tokens to his classmates if they were helpful or kind to him. One friend might get a token for carrying Lachlan's books, while another might get a token for sharing her lunch with Lachlan. Before too long, Lachlan's parents were contacted by the teacher because he had single-handedly demolished the teacher's classroom management strategy by introducing competition into the marketplace.

Such is the fragility of methods that come from the carrots and sticks manual.

Giving Up Control to Gain Control

Remember Shunryu Suzuki's advice from Chapter 6: 'To give your sheep or cow a large spacious meadow is the way to control him'. Suzuki was a clever guy. It just goes to show that some people have an intuitive sense of the idea of control before they even open a manual. Essentially, Suzuki seems to be saying that giving people what they want is the best way to control them. A control manual explains why this is such a sensible idea. It's sensible because people who are in control rarely if ever do the things that you don't want to see them do. As we learned earlier in the book, efforts to control people — especially efforts to control them arbitrarily without any concern for what they might want — result in conflict. People fight back against being controlled and this fighting back behavior can get pretty ugly. This is why carrot and stick control so often backfires. Suzuki realized that people who are in control — people who are able to get what they want — are people who are well-behaved. These people seem to be 'under control' because they are behaving exactly as you would like to see them behave. An even better way to follow Suzuki's advice would be to take the 'giver' out of the equation entirely, and to negotiate and organize environments so people can get what they want for themselves.

We hope this book will become something of a control manual for people who want to build a world worth the trouble. Once we recognize our controlling natures, building such a world becomes simple. Simple but not easy. Climbing the stairs and taking the view from the landing can reveal what needs to occur, but it can be difficult going back down the stairs and getting the job done.

Living with our own controlling nature will require a fundamental change to comfortable and well-worn ideas. Take the Golden Rule for example. We alluded to this rule in Chapter 3 but, at this stage of the book, it's appropriate to take a closer look. The Golden Rule is an ancient notion that embodies the ethic of *reciprocity*. The basic message is to do unto others as one would have done unto oneself, or, treat others the way you would like to be treated. Perhaps, by this stage of the book, you can see the flaws in the sentiment of this edict. If taken to its logical and literal extreme, it would create, rather than resolve, social discord. It is our contention that, even people who are fond of the Golden Rule, do not subscribe to its maxim on a daily basis.

If we were to follow the Golden Rule faithfully, we would strive to treat others the way we like to be treated. Let's say Hamish the office worker likes a double-shot espresso as his first cup of coffee in the morning. According to the Golden Rule, Hamish should serve his colleagues a double-shot espresso for their first cup of coffee because that would be treating people the way he likes to be treated. It is plain to see, however, that this is not how people act in social situations. Instead of giving people the coffee the way he likes it served, Hamish pays close to attention to the way others like their coffee served and he dishes it up that way. So Ariana gets the large Chai latte with no froth, Samuel gets the regular decaf flat white on Soy, and Jack gets the English Breakfast tea with one sugar.

This simple idea of giving people what they want applies generally. When we are buying birthday presents or gifts for any occasion we choose the gift based on what we think the other person will appreciate the most. On the whole, we do not buy gifts for others based on what we would like to receive, although sometimes, if we believe that our tastes are very similar to the other person's, we might use our preferences as a guide. The bottom line, however, is still a consideration of what the other person would like.

So, despite the longevity of the Golden Rule, it is not how people conduct their day to day affairs. Nor is it the ideal way to build lasting social harmony. The way people operate is very much in line with how the Golden Rule would be re-fashioned according to control principles. A Golden Rule from a control perspective would be: do unto others as they would have done unto themselves, or, treat other people the way they want to be treated.[3] We would argue this version of the Golden Rule is the 24 karat variety, whereas the Golden Rule currently doing the rounds is more of a Fool's Gold version because it maps so poorly onto the way we are designed.

Rising Above the Desire to Control Others

Living with our own controlling nature, therefore, involves recognizing that we will, from time to time, want to control other people. Getting chummy with our controllingness will also mean acknowledging the problems that trying to control other people will inevitably create. Paradoxically, by giving others the freedom to have the control they want, we will actually be giving ourselves more freedom as well.

Controlling other people not only restricts the range of their controlling efforts, it also restricts our controlling. More than anything, we need to appreciate our own controlling natures because that will be good for us. It will have pay-offs for others too, but the main beneficiaries will be ourselves. From this perspective, a control manual helps us understand that *altruism* is, ultimately, a selfish act. People who are altruistic act this way because it is the way they like to be. It is part of their controlling nature to tirelessly help other people and to put the needs of others before their own. Conducting themselves in this way helps them make their worlds be right. It may seem strange at first to think about altruism in this way but these kinds of topsy-turvy surprises are commonplace when one starts reading from a control manual.

Another prevailing idea that would undergo an overhaul in a control manual is the attitude of 'walking a mile in another person's shoes'. There's a joke based on this idea that suggests that before you criticize another person you should walk a mile in their shoes so that, when you've finished criticizing them, you will be a mile away from them and you will have their shoes! All jokes aside, coming to grips with our controlling natures will help us understand that we can never walk a mile, or any distance at all, in another person's shoes. We can never experience what it is to be another person. We can listen to people, and we can think about how we might feel in a similar situation, but we can never be that other person or experience what they experience.

Recognizing that we will never know the experiences of others turns out to be a very useful perspective to adopt. It means that we can stop *assuming* we know why people do certain things and we can develop an ongoing curiosity about the things that people control. From this point of view we might take more interest in the things that others control and become more of a help and less of a hindrance to their controlling ways.

Understanding that our own experiences are unique also clarifies why fashioning a world worth the trouble is so imperative. It is because the world worth the trouble is our world. It is Rick's world, it is Tim's world, it is your world. We each have our own worlds that we carry around in our heads. Our day-to-day business involves acting on the world 'out there' to keep our inside world the way we want it to be. That is the very essence of control. Ghandi's quote that 'We must be the change we wish to see in the world"[4] is especially relevant here. The world that is worth the trouble is the world that each of us is creating for ourselves as we go about our controlling business. Being the change we want to see in the world means recognizing the controlling we do, and the controlling done by others, and understanding what it means to live with our controlling nature.

So that's it. We control. In fact every living creature controls. We can't ever stop controlling but we can change what we control. More specifically, we can change the focus of our controlling efforts. Just like a line of falling dominoes, what we are currently controlling is connected in a very real way to other unseen controlled experiences further up the line. We are always attending to the control of some aspects of our world in order to keep other, invisible aspects of the world the way we need them to be. As Ellie kneels down to put petrol in the lawn mower she might not, at that time, be aware that controlling the amount of petrol in the mower's tank and minimizing the amount that sloshes down the outside is helping her control the appearance of the front lawn, which helps her control the pride she has in her house, which helps her control the sense she has of being a good neighbor and citizen, which helps her control her view of herself as she likes to be. That's a lot of controlling from one little top up of petrol. While Ellie is intently watching the flow of petrol she is probably not thinking about the type of citizen she is but that important control structure is there nevertheless.

We are only ever aware of a tiny portion of the inner world we are controlling at any point in time. Becoming familiar with different tiles in the controlling mosaic that is who we are will help us live more comfortably and contentedly in a world that is undoubtedly worth the trouble. Understanding our controlling nature won't turn our day-to day humdrum into

Disneyland or transport us to a place beyond the rainbow. It certainly won't make all of our problems and daily hassles disappear. It is precisely because we are controlling creatures that we will constantly be buffeted, knocked, and jostled as we go about our business. By keeping a control manual tucked under our arm, however, we will be able to navigate the bumps and collisions far more efficiently than ever before.

Getting In Touch with your Controlling Nature

One thing we will learn as we digest the control manual is that many of life's travesties we actually create for ourselves in the landscapes of our minds. This is not to discount that crummy things can happen to a person in life but the way we keep company with that crumminess depends very much upon our own controlling proclivities. While Tom controls the rate at which an important work report is completed he might become increasingly irritated at his young son Finn's repeated requests to read the next chapter of 'Treasure Island' together. Because Tom has studied a control manual, however, it won't be too long before he realizes that Finn is not the source of the irritation. Tom wants to get the report finished but he also wants to be a good dad. His irritation arises as he focusses on controlling two experiences that, at this particular moment, are incompatible.

Being well versed in the mechanics of his controlling nature, Tom recognizes that there are other controlled states that he needs to bring into view. He decides to climb the stairs to the landing, no, to the upstairs balcony, for a bird's eye view of the situation. From this loftier vantage point he sees that he wants to control the completion rate of the report because he is controlling his perfect record of meeting deadlines at work which helps him control his success at work which helps him control his career progression. On thinking about his career progression, it occurs to him that his career progression helps him control the extent to which he provides for his family. Aha! Almost at the same time that providing for his family comes into view, it dawns on Tom that providing emotionally for his family is just as important to him as providing financially. Tom's irritation melts away and, as he snuggles closer to Finn on the sofa to find out about young Jim Hawkins' latest exploits, it crosses his mind that a break from the report will actually be helpful, and when he returns to it he knows he'll be able to swiftly wrap it up.

Tom's lesson here is instructive. Whenever we are feeling irascible or out of sorts, it can pay big dividends to reflect on the controlling we are doing at that particular time. The more quickly we can climb the stairs for a better view, the more short-lived our grumpiness will be. Moreover we will have learned a little more about the things in life that are important to us.

If humanity is to reach adolescence, we need to relish our controlling nature. By controlling the world around us we have created trinkets of great beauty and structures of mind-boggling size and shape. We can situate large chunks of metal in the sky and move them around the globe. We can send people to the moon or deep into the ocean. We can cure hideous diseases and mend broken bones. Still we find it hard to decide whose turn it is to do the washing up or to shrug off the jerk who just cut in front of us on the freeway.

Control is the way it is. Life is control. We need to understand it, and we need to learn to live with it. We need to strive for a world where people prioritize finding ways to control what is important to themselves in a way that minimizes the extent to which they interfere with the controlling of others.

That, and all that it implies, would really be a world worth the trouble.

Endnotes

Preface

1 First edition published 1973 by Aldine; second edition published 2005 by Benchmark Publications.

Chapter 1

1 Skinner, B.F. (1981). Selection by Consequences, *Science, 213*, 501–504.

2 Skinner, B.F. (1985). *A Matter of Consequences (B.F. Skinner's Autobiography, Pt 3)* New York University Press.

3 Skinner, B.F. (1972). *Beyond Freedom and Dignity*, New York: Bantam Vintage.

4 The story was told to the first author in an undergraduate psychology course, around the time that the Skinner-Fromm encounter occurred, which speaks more to the age of the first author than the veracity of the story.

5 Skinner, B.F. (1972) *Beyond Freedom and Dignity*, New York: Bantam Vintage. p. 166.

6 We learned about our nature as controlling people when we first read Powers's classic, but highly technical, text on the subject: *Behavior: The Control of Perception*. Chicago-Aldine, 1973; 2nd edition Benchmark Publications, 2005.

7 A paraphrase of what is now known as the serenity prayer, attributed to Reinhold Niebuhr, from *We Plan Our Own Worship Services*, by Winnifred Crane Wygal.

Chapter 2

1   Weisman, A. (2007). *The World Without Us*, New York: St. Martin's Press

2   James, W. (1890). *The Principles of Psychology.* New York: Dover.

3   James, W. (1890). *The Principles of Psychology.* New York: Dover. p. 7

Chapter 3

1   Powers, W. T. (1973). *Behavior: The control of perception.* Chicago: Aldine.

2   Heider, F, & Simmel, M. (1944). An experimental study of apparent behavior. *American Journal of Psychology, 57,* 243–259.

3   Powers, W. T. (1973). Feedback: Beyond behaviorism. Science, 179, 351-356. Reprinted in Powers, W. T. (1989). *Living Control Systems. Selected Papers of William T. Powers* (pp. 61-78). Benchmark Publications, Bloomfield, NJ. www.benchpress.com/Books2.htm978-0-9647121-3-3 (paperback)

Chapter 4

1   Whitman, W. *Song of Myself.*

2   Hawking, S. (1988). *A Brief History of Time.* Bantam Books.

Chapter 5

1   Pirsig, R. (1973). *Zen and the Art of Motorcycle Maintenance,* Bantam.

2   http://www.mindreadings.com/ControlDemo/Select.html

3   The control hierarchy is 'to some extent' responsible for keeping intrinsic variables at their reference level because there are also physiological mechanisms at work as well. So besides how we dress, body temperature also depends on physiological actions such as sweating and constriction of capillaries.

4   Dylan, B. *Too much of nothing*, Dwarf Music, copyright 1998.

Chapter 6

1   http://www.goodreads.com/author/quotes/62707.Shunryu_Suzuki

Chapter 8

www.methodoflevels.com.au

Chapter 10

1   Powers, W. T. (1997). email to CSGNET; Subject: Re: Going up a level (970617/0812 MDT).

2   Which is the same as the rewards and punishments or rein-forcements and withholding reinforcements manual.

3   Robertson, R.J., & Powers, W.T. (Eds.). (1990). *Introduction to modern psychology: The control-theory view.* New Canaan, CT: Benchmark Publications

4   http://www.brainyquote.com/quotes/authors/m/mahatma_gandhi.html

CPSIA information can be obtained at www.ICGtesting.com
Printed in the USA
BVOW08s1450231215

430904BV00001B/29/P